sanctuary

Sun
Compassion
Wisdom
Meaning
Understanding
Intimacy
Ambiguity
Discovery
Wonder
Earth
Waves
Stars
Planets
Rain
Fire
Gales
Ice
Flames
Moon
Circles
Sky
Mist
Friends
Wit
Flowers
Books
Mind
Letters
Connecting
Miracles
Love
Silver
Garden
Candle light
Shabbos
Hugs
Soul
Strangers
Trees
Touch
Dreaming
Beach
Words
Laughter
Kindness
Paint
Music
Skin
Birds
Snow
Soil
Song
Hearts
Cats
Piano
Art
Dark
Bed
Light
Poetry

sanctuary

the discovery *of* wonder

Julie Leibrich

OTAGO

To the community of Southern Star Abbey, Kopua

Published by Otago University Press
Level 1, 398 Cumberland Street
Dunedin, New Zealand
university.press@otago.ac.nz
www.otago.ac.nz/press

First published 2015

ISBN 978-1-877578-96-0

The author and publisher gratefully acknowledge the permission granted to reproduce the copyright material in this book. Every effort has been made to trace copyright holders and to obtain their permission for the use of copyright material. The publisher apologises for any errors or omissions in the above list and would be grateful if notified of any corrections that should be incorporated in future reprints or editions of this book.

Published with the assistance of Creative New Zealand

creative nz
ARTS COUNCIL OF NEW ZEALAND TOI AOTEAROA

A catalogue record for this book is available from the National Library of New Zealand.

Publisher: Rachel Scott
Editor: Emma Neale
Design/layout: Fiona Moffat

Cover/frontispiece: *The Space within the Heart* by Julie Leibrich.
Black ink and watercolour on paper, 420 x 590 mm

Printed in China through Asia Pacific Offset Ltd

contents

wondering about sanctuary

A web of ideas: fragile links with strong connections, Kopua 2011.

a space for ideas

It's hard to say exactly when this book began, but it was about the time I scribbled a note and pinned it to the wall of my studio. That was 10 years ago and the note is still there:

> There has been a space for a long time now – a vacancy for something that matters. I find cryptic notes in folders saying 'The Book', 'A Book of Discovery'. It keeps turning up on 'To Do' lists and 'Projects for the Year' and keeps sliding off. It's so hard to protect space. Bold brash things jut in and nudge out nothingness. Yet I need nothing. I need the *absence* of noise and light and clutter. I need space.

At the time I wrote that note, I needed somewhere to put my thoughts – a place where I could find them easily in case I forgot them, somewhere safe, somewhere outside the instability of my mind. Eventually, I found a box that I wanted to keep notes in and it became a place for ideas that mattered to me.

Once we start being deeply aware of something, we meet it everywhere. We bump into it on street corners, see it out of the corner of our eye. We start to notice it in different places and disguises. Maybe it even starts to notice us. Maybe it comes calling?

I would write something in a letter to a friend or in a journal and think, 'That should be in the book.' I would read something and think, 'Exactly! I must remember to mention that.' Or I would have to scribble down something someone said in a conversation.

Journal, October 2008

I have been looking for sanctuary all my life, as if I were living The Great Escape. *But escape from what? Contact with others, spotlights, narrowness? At sixty, I think I have found sanctuary at last. Well, a kind of sanctuary – one that will do in the meantime.*

Piles of paper, scribbled notes and crumpled photographs stack up in different corners of my life. There has to be a time of gathering yet I avoid it. Maybe I am frightened that if I try to catch the thoughts they will disappear. Perhaps they are fluff and nonsense anyway.

There is only one way to find out. That is to write. So today, I open my Book of Sanctuary.

I had entered a long, absorbing contemplation on sanctuary. The word sanctuary comes from the Latin word *sanctus*, which means holy. Later it came to be used to mean refuge, a place of safety. The word contemplation comes from the Latin words *con*, meaning with and *templus* meaning temple. In Ancient Rome, the *templus* was a sacred space used by a priest to observe the heavens and interpret the will of the gods. So contemplation, in a sense, means gazing from a sacred space.

Much of the time my contemplation was passive. I contemplated sanctuary *within* sanctuary. I sat alone and still, listening to silence. I became conscious of the space between day and night, night and day, and more aware of ideas that came to me in dreams.

At other times contemplation was active. I revisited books and articles I had written, to find clues about my past understanding of sanctuary. I reviewed my journals and poems to find experiences of sanctuary. I looked at photographs, listened to music, read old letters. I relived past experiences, lived in the present moment, and tried to imagine futures as I thought about what sanctuary really meant to me. I thought about the many ways in which I find sanctuary in the physical world and contemplated the sanctuary that exists within myself. Most of all, I kept thinking about the connection between sanctuary within and without.

Pages and chapters emerged over about five years. I saw the completed book in my mind many times, though it often changed shape. Gradually, writing the book became a sanctuary in itself. I wasn't sure how, but I knew that writing about sanctuary was transforming me, making me feel whole.

I asked friends and acquaintances what the word sanctuary meant to them. I widened my discussions and, in the end, asked over a hundred people if they could describe an *experience* of sanctuary. I wanted to deepen my personal understanding, not gather material for sociological analysis. I soon realised that I was finding treasure for general reflection, so later asked people for permission to share their thoughts in this book. These are presented in an appendix: Glimpses of Sanctuary. Some quotations accompany my own text because they particularly spoke to me or said something much better than I could say it.

When I asked people what the word sanctuary meant to them, most described places or people that made them feel safe and free. They talked of activities, or states of mind, or spiritual experiences which brought them strength, ease, and a sense of the sacredness of life. They remembered times of serenity, tranquillity.

Every time someone told me what sanctuary meant to him or her, the meaning seemed to shift a little. I would see a shadowy shape in the distance and, as I got closer, it would take a different form before my eyes. I would walk away, to refocus at a distance, but when I turned around, it had altered yet again. I began to wonder if sanctuary were a chimera. Maybe it meant everything, and so, in a way, nothing? Gradually, I came to see that sanctuary is a shape-shifter, which changes according to our needs and stage of life, and according to opportunities. Most of all, what sanctuary seemed to be about was giving people the time and space they need to be who they really are.

Other writers were a source of company and I had imaginary conversations with people whose work inspires me. Words themselves were a crucial part of contemplation. I would spend days thinking about an individual word, carrying it around with me, savouring it on my tongue. I looked up words the way we look up old friends, but tracked them down in dictionaries and etymologies. I painted them and played with them. I often sat in silence, repeating a word slowly in my mind. Sometimes I tried to become nothing but the word.

If I were an artist, I would paint sanctuary. If I were a composer, I would write a symphony about it. If I were a mathematician, I would construct a conjecture about it. As a writer all I can do is search for words, or wait until they find me.

Ideas are not straight, tidy things, boxed up like birthday presents. Not at all. They are dishevelled things, or angry things, or ghosts whispering behind curtains. Sometimes we have to dig deep into the earth to find them. Sometimes they seem to drop from the sky. I often have to wait for feelings to catch up with thinking, or vice versa.

My vagabond brain is always wandering and wondering. Often when I wonder about something, and wander around it, I come to wonder at it. That process of wondering, wandering and wonderment has been at the heart of this entire contemplation. Maybe it is all of these things?

Questioning becomes marvelling. Do we discover sanctuary or does it uncover us? Is sanctuary outside or within us or does it dissolve such boundaries? Is sanctuary somewhere to go or something to become?

My cultural heritage underpins everything I write. My language is English, my day-to-day world is small and my knowledge of religion is mainly of Christianity and Judaism. I am keenly aware of my limitations and they became clearer at every turn, while writing this book.

There is no advice in this book as I am no expert about sanctuary, just someone who happens to have been thinking about it for a long time. I hope that you will find things here that lead you into wondering, wandering and wonderment.

In this section, 'Wondering about Sanctuary', I have explained how I came to write this book. Next, I will talk about why I needed to discover sanctuary.

The second section, 'Illuminating Sanctuary', illustrates the sanctuary we find in places, people, mind, body and spirit, and most importantly, by taking time for time.

The third section, 'Protecting Sanctuary', explores the need to look after the sanctuary within by making space for space. It discusses social ambivalence towards solitude, silence, simplicity, slowness and stillness, and describes the fears and joys of experiencing them.

The fourth section, 'Wonderment of

Sanctuary' looks at the relationship between mystery, meaning and miracle. It suggests that when a mystery is given personal meaning, it can become a miracle, and that sanctuary itself is a miracle that renews life.

The contemplation then draws to a close, concluding that when we strengthen and protect the sanctuary in ourselves, we can relate more authentically and show greater compassion for others.

Danger sign. Waikanae, 2011.

a story of discovery

You have to begin with the knowledge that there is nothing perfect in this world. Our job is not to hunt down perfection and live within it. It is to take whatever broken pieces we have found and sew them together as best we can.

THE REBBE[1]

Not long after I turned 30, depression overwhelmed me and I spent several months in a psychiatric hospital. While I was in hospital, my first husband formed a relationship with someone else and left me. Not long afterwards, I lost my home, connection with many friends and the community in which I had lived.

A few weeks after leaving hospital, I tried to take my own life and was admitted to a psychiatric ward in another hospital. I felt as if I did not belong to myself any longer: I had locked myself out of myself.

It was the beginning of a new decade and it seemed crucial not to be in a psychiatric hospital on New Year's Day. Against medical advice, I discharged myself on New Year's Eve and was warned that if I had further problems, I would be committed. It was a very frightening prospect, but my determination to leave hospital was a major turning point in my life. I had an enormous resolve to survive, which became my renewal.

At some point during the next few months, I came across a book by Aubrey Menen called *The Space Within the Heart*.[2] He asked the question: when everything is peeled away – our environment, history, pretences, masks, constructions of the world – what is left? Facing this question for himself had taken him to a major turning point in his life. He stopped, made space, confronted the truth about himself and discovered what mattered in his life. He found 'the space within the heart' as described in the collection of spiritual writings that inspired him – *The Upanishads*, the founding text of Hinduism, compiled about 2500 years ago.[3]

A single idea can change a person's entire life. Just as *The Upanishads* had changed Menen's life, so his book changed mine. Very slowly, I began to treasure my essence, my *being*, the breath of life, the innermost part of me, my core – my soul.

Gradually, I made a life for myself again. I finished my PhD and began work as a research psychologist. Not long after, I remarried. Yet, although I had *heard* what Menen had said about the space within the heart, I had not embodied it. I had hardly learnt how to enter the space within my heart, and certainly not how to stay there. The next few years were difficult and my second husband, Doug Harvie, and I separated. We lived alone but close by each other and we remained loving friends.

While working for the Justice Department, I wrote my first book, *Straight to the Point: Angles on giving up crime*.[4] I had wanted to find out why people with criminal careers give up crime. I talked, at length, with individuals who had a criminal record but who seemed to have stopped offending. Some had grown tired or grown out of criminal activities, but others talked about *deciding* to go straight. They described, sometimes explicitly, a turning point in their lives. They had found a job or met someone they came to love, or become a parent. They had begun to take responsibility for their behaviour, sometimes experiencing great shame and remorse.

They began to renew themselves, for instance by confronting addiction, or by moving away from a particular circle of friends, or by making a commitment to a partner.[5] They changed their behaviour only when life was meaningful enough for them to *want* to go straight. It was like a light going on for them.

A light went on in me too. Towards the end of writing *Going Straight* I was walking on the beach one day and had a vision. I looked back over my shoulder down the beach and saw myself, at the end of a long line in the sand, at the age of 80. I said to this older self, 'You can't wait for me any longer, I'll come now.' I knew that I had to start being true to myself – now! That was a life-changing realisation.

Up till then, I had never been committed to life. Now, I began to see some point in living. I saw things I wanted to do *now*. I always knew, for example, that I was a writer, but I had never acknowledged that. Now writing became an integral part of my life.

Continuing to work as a research psychologist, I studied family violence, but found this unbearably stressful work. During this time, I spoke about my experiences as a psychiatric patient for the first time to others and before long was invited to give the academic address at the annual conference of the Australian and New Zealand College of Psychiatrists.[6] I realised that many people were affected by my talk, but I had no idea how deeply affected I would be myself. That day, I heard myself speak words that I had buried inside me for a long time.

At that time, I was still ashamed of having been diagnosed with a 'mental illness'. I had not only been shamed by society but had internalised that shame. The problem with shame is that it makes you cover up your true self, and you're not authentic any more. Shame becomes sham. It was not until I uncovered and acknowledged my *own* shame that I was free of it.

Two years later I became a Mental Health Commissioner for New Zealand. One of my tasks was to work towards reducing discrimination against people diagnosed with a 'mental illness'. In my fourth year as Commissioner I wrote a book based on interviews with people about how they managed their experience of illness. Twenty-one people, myself included, shared their personal story about dealing with illness in ways that meant we lived our lives to the fullest. Our hope was to educate people and so reduce discrimination, and help others manage their own illness. *A Gift of Stories: Discovering how to deal with mental illness* was published 20 years, almost to the day, after I had discharged myself from a psychiatric ward. As I said there, 'I finished this book amazed by the ability of human beings to overcome adversity and discover new life.'[7] The book has travelled far, been used widely, and inspired other, similar books.[8]

Stories share much more than ideas. When we listen to a story carefully our spirit, intellect and feelings are as one so that the story has the power to *touch* us. A story gives us the chance to understand something by standing under it – and allowing us to see it from a new perspective.

Not long after the book was released, my own life took yet another turn. I had allowed my job as Commissioner to take over and found my working world so crowded, fast, complicated, noisy and frantic that I unravelled. I had not protected the space within my own heart. Clearly, I was due for another lesson about making space.

It came in the form of serious illness. Brain scans indicated neurological disease, which the neurologist said might be multiple sclerosis or an early dementia. He advised me to retire immediately. For about a year, I merely existed. I used up my savings then went on an invalid's benefit for another year. I felt washed up onto a shore after years of being at sea. I was exhausted and battered, but was coming home and was safe. It was a very slow re-integration to become authentic again. I was returning to my true self. I was becoming real.

In a children's story by Margery Williams Bianco, two toys, the Skin Horse and the Rabbit, talk about becoming real:

> 'Does it hurt?' asked the Rabbit.
>
> 'Sometimes,' said the Skin Horse, for he was always truthful. 'When you are Real, you don't mind being hurt.'
>
> 'Does it happen all at once, like being wound up?' he asked, 'or bit by bit?'
>
> 'It doesn't happen all at once,' said the Skin Horse. 'You *become*. It takes a long time. That's why it doesn't often happen to people who break easily, or have sharp edges, or who have to be carefully kept. Generally by the time you're Real, most of your hair has been loved off, and your eyes drop out and you get loose in the jowls and very shabby. But these things don't matter at all, because once you are Real, you can't be ugly, except to people who don't understand.'[9]

If I think about that period of illness now, I would say that slowing down gave me the chance to heal. Before I retired I was like a satellite speeding round a lifeless planet. I had tried to slow down but it wasn't until I retired that I began to succeed. I had to stop before I could even think about *how* to slow down. I may not grasp some things as quickly as I did back then but I think I understand them more deeply. Ideas don't have to travel at the speed of light to shine.

About a year after I retired, I was invited to the World Assembly for Mental Health in Canada to give the Mary Hemingway Rees Memorial Lecture, an address dedicated to 'mental health and spirituality'.[10] As I was still very ill, it seemed an impossible challenge. Yet I had such a strong intuition that I was meant to do this and that I would somehow be helped, that I said yes. Accepting the invitation was one of the most significant turning points in my life. I had faith by then that the words would find me.

In one moment, on one night, for reasons we cannot articulate, our world spins round on a new axis. We might *feel* the change inside, as if something is shifting within our core, but we may not know what is going on. Usually, we don't recognise a turning point when it happens. We may not realise the significance of an event or an experience at the time and may only see it later, when we reflect on that period of our life.

When I accepted the invitation to write about 'mental health and spirituality', I recognised, for the first time in my life, a turning point *as it was happening*. For years, I hadn't talked about my spiritual beliefs. I hadn't even articulated them to myself. They were there, but fuzzy things inside me, vague feelings, strange experiences, echoes from some past heritage I felt I had, certainly not formed in the shape of beliefs and practices. My spiritual life began to become clearer to me, and I very slowly began to find the confidence to acknowledge it.

Journal, May 2001

Everything seems altered. I have been in such a 'reflective' stage of my life that I have found any outside contacts very difficult. I have been drinking silence and solitude with an incredible thirst.

My spiritual growth has been paramount and led me to a reclusive state. I have been so overwhelmed with the wonder of the world. At times, I am not sure if my experiences have been magical, manic or mystical. I think the latter.

Amazing dreams and experiences of the world leave me in no doubt that there is a God. Something far beyond me that makes me feel connected to the universe and gives me someone to talk to and pray to. This has become crucial for me.

In his reflections on *Yom Kippur*, the most sacred day in the Jewish calendar, Chief Rabbi Sir Jonathan Sacks writes:

> Crisis forces us to make difficult but necessary decisions. It makes us ask, 'Who am I and what really matters to me?' It plunges us from the surface to the depths, where we discover strengths we didn't know we had, and a clarity of purpose we had hitherto lacked. So you have to say to every crisis, 'I will not let you go until you bless me.'[11]

In the lecture I gave in Canada, *Making Space: Spirituality and mental health*, I argued that health means being whole and that, when ill, it is less easy to see ourselves as whole. Given that one of the most devastating experiences of 'mental illness' is that very *sense* of not being whole – the disintegration of self – any therapy that treats a person in a disintegrated way is not just ineffective, it is harmful because it reinforces the fragmentation of illness. It erodes a person's innate power to heal.

I then focused on the importance of spirituality in dealing with my own 'mental illness' and said that I experience spirituality as space:

> I call it the space within my heart. It's the place where I meet myself. It's where I belong. It is where I find a sense of deeper connection – with myself, and with something beyond myself – a spirit greater than myself. And sometimes, very occasionally, a connection with another person, who is standing in *their* space.
>
> It is the space I go into when I need to find meaning in my life, when I need to come to terms with life or death, or when I need to accept that nothing stays the same. It's where I go when I need to cope with the knowledge that I walk alone in this world, or experience the comfort of infinite love.
>
> It is the space between reason and imagination. Space where time is in a different perspective, where things I could not have predicted happen. Space where I feel loved, where I feel at peace, where I discover things. It is a kind of coming home. For me, the meaning of spirituality is meaning itself.[12]

While writing the talk, I made a very important reconnection with my past. I had been searching for a translation of work by Henri Baruk, the French neuropsychiatrist who had given the second Rees Hemingway Memorial Lecture, in 1960, in Edinburgh. The only comprehensive translation I could find turned out to be by an old friend, Barry Lent, whom I had not heard of for 40 years.[13] A childhood memory flashed back: a Friday night meal in their home, when they lit candles and said prayers.

After reading my lecture, my friend sent me the next book that was to change my life. Its title was *Toward a Meaningful Life: The wisdom of the Rebbe*, gathered by Rabbi Simon Jacobson.[14]

Once the talk was published, many people of like mind contacted me and we formed relationships that continue to be deeply meaningful in my life. Two years later I was invited to a mental health conference in Melbourne to give an address about spiritual life. I explained there that I needed to be still: to be *at home* with myself.[15]

It was about this time that I began to acknowledge my yearning to find out more about Judaism. The poet and lay theologian G.K. Chesterton had a brilliant phrase for not knowing or living one's spiritual beliefs – he called it being 'homesick at home'.[16] If there were any one phrase I would choose to describe the last 10 years of my life, it would be this: *I came home.* There are no records that show my ancestors were Jewish, yet I have always *felt* that they were.

I began to read and became immersed in the ideas of Jewish thought. One of the most important steps I took was to join a weekly class in New York via the internet. The richness and emotional depth of the classes run by Rabbi Simon Jacobson was immense for me. And it was through this that I found the courage to speak of my life-long 'sense of Jewishness' to friends. I began to observe *Shabbat*. This is the Hebrew word for the Jewish Sabbath. There is a Yiddish word for it too, *Shabbos*, which is the word I remember from childhood and use myself. One by one I learned about the Jewish *chagim* (festivals) and I began to learn Hebrew. As the American author Herman Wouk says, 'You can listen to a hundred lectures and read 40 books on what Judaism is, and learn less than you can by carrying out in a single year the duties and the pleasures of the festivals.'[17]

A basic difficulty for me, which I have not yet resolved, is that Judaism is first and foremost a religion of community and practice – as most religions are – but I am by nature reclusive. I realised that I had to be authentic if I were to answer the calling of my soul. Slowly, I began take steps towards this – wherever and however they led. I also knew, deep down, that what I wanted was not a religion but a relationship with God.

One of the most important steps for me was to find a place of retreat, a place where I felt completely safe and sacred, and where I could take the time to find the qualities of safety and sacredness within myself. For me, this place was a Trappist monastery, with a magnetic spiritual presence, on a remote country road, removed from the everyday world.

Journal, September 2002, Kopua

After nearly two years of longing to go on retreat and searching for somewhere I finally found Kopua. Getting here seemed so easy. A simple phone call. A yes. The long easy drive from Raumati, across the straights of the Manawatu, into the Hawke's Bay.

Why have I come? To be still and to listen. To rest. To step off the treadmill for a while and be among others and yet be safely alone.

When I stand still, it's usually sadness that reaches me, or do I reach sadness?

I have made rituals of nothing, focused on the meaning of zero, and lived life by measuring death. In the waiting room there are no walls, no door. The space is an arm's reach from the heart.

I am so afraid to live. I am so afraid of pain that I have become it. I have been a bystander most of my life. Not a 'belonger'. What if tears are a sign of life? They prove I can be touched, loved, warmed, affected, and have feeling.

The monks remind themselves by chanting six times a day. It is part of the daily practice. I need this too. A daily practice. Today I am going to look for prayers and begin to write them in a prayer book. It might go on for a long time. I want to learn how to pray.

Sometimes, these days, I don't recognise myself any more. Who am I now? I am not sure if my quiet is from my heart or my head. Born of health or born of illness.

In his sermon, the Abbot said the task is to love ourselves, to love others, and to love God – in that order.

To love myself is the hardest thing in the world. That is what makes me rattle with emptiness. I am a hollow woman. How can I love others unless I love myself? It is from this place that I need to begin and I suppose all hangs on the belief that God loves me.

If God loves me, then how could I not love myself? I need that belief to survive. I also need to believe I have some purpose on earth. Not some great goal at some unknown end-point, but something that makes dailiness meaningful.

I feel a breath of air in a windless courtyard. What do you want me to do?

Keep writing.

But do not dwell in the words.

Let the words dwell in you, let them dissolve in you.

I had found something that I been searching for all my life, even though I had not known what it was. It was only at that moment that I knew what I had been looking for and the word that came to my lips was sanctuary.

illuminating sanctuary

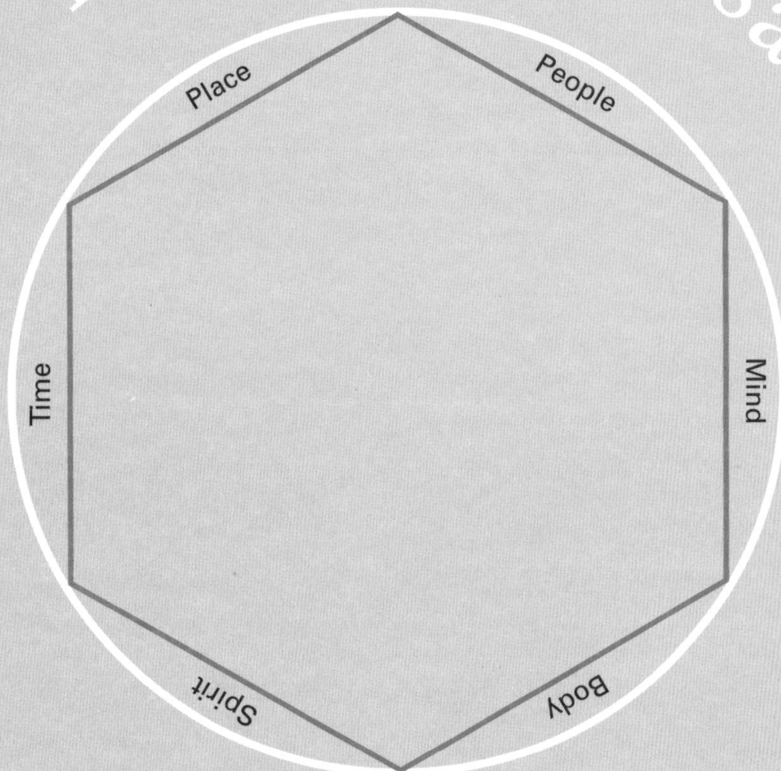

I was taking a photograph of this lovely old shed in a small town in the South Island, when a little boy walked into the picture. Clearly, he belonged in this place. Clyde, 2006.

belonging of place

The sanctuary of homeland

The north of England was my first home, the one that made me as I am. People from Lancashire pride themselves on being blunt and knowing how to face adversity. I love the north and always will. It's like a friend who knew me as a child and my relationship with it is deeper for that. I want and need to stay connected to the north. I have gone back nearly 20 times since I came to New Zealand; I collect books and pictures of the places I lived in as a child; I listen to the music of that time and place. I still get homesick for the north.

When I was in my twenties I travelled around the world and eventually settled in New Zealand. It took a long time to see it as home. Can we come home to somewhere we are not from? Yes, I think immigrants do it all the time. Safety, acceptance and opportunity: these things make a country a home, a sanctuary. Eventually, I found all of these in New Zealand.

It is customary for Māori to introduce themselves on a marae with a mihimihi (brief talk). They identify themselves by the geographic features associated with their tribe: maunga (mountain), awa (river) and moana (sea). If I were to give a mihimihi I would say, 'I come from the Pennine range, my River is the Irwell, my sea is the Tasman, and my island is Kapiti.'

The sanctuary of home

Home is where I can be myself – no pretence, no best behaviour, who I *really* am. It is the place of greatest familiarity, the place that stokes me up, by heart and hearth. Home is the only place where I can reliably go in and close the door on the world, if I need to. Warmth, ease, safety, privacy, peace, comfort, being myself, being with someone I love, and also having the chance for some solitude – this is the meaning of home to me. It's where I long to be, so it's where I belong.

The owner of a local café expresses the relief and safety of just being at home:

> Sanctuary is being safe, comfortable and secure. It's a lovely word. I have sanctuary just about every night when I go home. Six days a week I am at the café, not only at the café but front of house at the café. That means I can't hide (in the kitchen where no one can see me). I have to be bright, cheery, healthy, happy, clean, helpful, kind, caring, courteous, welcoming, funny, patient (just to name a few). Home is sanctuary to me because I can be myself without having to 'pretend' to be any of those things I have just mentioned.
>
> BARBARA FLEMING

At home, we have a large garden, where I can lose myself or find myself. In the northwest corner of the garden is a place I call 'The Sanctuary'. It is a secluded, private area around a walnut tree and has a door that I can close and lock. A *sense* of enclosure can enhance beauty. In spring, The Sanctuary has a carpet of plum blossom, followed by violets and bluebells, foxgloves and columbine. In summer, the scents of jasmine and lemon balm fill the air, and the leaves in the walnut tree make a cool, green canopy. By the end of autumn, I am gathering walnuts, just before the garden retreats into the dark loam of winter.

The *act* of enclosing something can make it secret and sacred. In religion and art, the Garden of Eden represents protection, innocence, beginnings. The root of the word Paradise means enclosure - 'a wall around'. I first learnt about the significance of walled gardens while studying Mediaeval English. We had a delightful professor, who enthralled us with his descriptions of rituals and symbols, courtly love and cloisters, anchorite nuns and mystics. The concept of an enclosed garden symbolised so much about mediaeval thinking – the magic dance between safety, secrecy and sacredness.

In *The Allegory of Love: A study of love in mediaeval tradition*, C.S. Lewis explains that the act of love itself is not merely set within enclosed gardens, but symbolised by them. One of the most famous thirteenth-century texts, the *Roman de la Rose*, in which courtship is set in a walled garden, illuminates the mediaeval concept that the interior world represents romance while the exterior represents ordinary life.

The sanctuary of nature

When I lived in Britain, the places that made me feel at one with the universe were the moors of Lancashire and Yorkshire. I loved the freedom and space and I belonged to that land. In New Zealand I find those feelings on the beach near where we live and that I walk along almost every day. I have loved there, laughed there and grieved there. I have fun there, swim in the sea there, write poems there, and take my worries there. The sea never turns its back on me.

Water can distil us. It is the purest form of life. In spring, I go down to meet showers and rainbows. In summer I walk barefoot, splashing in the lightness of being. In autumn, the northwesterlies thrill me with their turbulence. This is the season I walk at sunset, to get close to the embers of day. In winter I walk around noon, bundled up in my coat and scarf to face the icy southerlies.

When I walk on the beach, just as when I work in the garden, I am aware of seasons yet unaware of time. I see things differently on the beach. It's as if the perspective inside me mirrors the one I am seeing outside, and is wider, and focused further away. Things become clear walking on a beach. The waves jostle questions until solutions stand out against the light, like silhouettes.

As a beach-walker on a western coast, you see the full moon set at sunrise, and the newish moon set at sunset. You notice how the setting sun shifts sideways along the horizon as the seasons change. You come to believe you can read the weather in the clouds. You long to see what the latest storm has brought in on the high tide. You watch the sand levels rise and fall. You stare and count the waves, waiting for the big one. You go down at night in the gales of the equinox to see king tides. You are part of a nodding, waving community that provides easy companionship. You recognise people who walk the same route and feel at home with them. Particular dogs become special friends. You get to know gulls intimately. You know the kahawai are running when you see a cloud of gulls over the water. You save bread for the oystercatchers and wait for the terns to return from the other side of the world.

The sanctuary of remote places

As a girl, I spent hours poring over maps of remote places, wanting to be a pirate and planning routes across the seven seas. What pirates did for a living seemed irrelevant. I just wanted to sail around the world. I remember spending a whole weekend with my friend Chrissie at her auntie's house. All we did was plan our route to the Caribbean. It wasn't play at all to me – I believed it would happen.

Next, spellbound by Jules Verne's *A Journey to the Centre of the Earth,* I marked my exact entry point on a map of Iceland, made detailed lists of provisions for the journey and began to save up for 4000 miles of rope. It sounds absurd now, yet at nine years old I was convinced it was possible to go down a volcano and reach the centre of the world. Moreover, that quite soon, I would do exactly that.

I also dreamt about exploring the Arctic and the Equator; as now I dream of going to the Antarctic. Almost always, though, islands have been the focus of my longings. What is it about an island that so arouses the imagination?

When we remember our childhood dreams and longings, I wonder if the path our adult life has taken makes more sense? During my contemplation on the sanctuary of places, I came to see that so many choices I made in adult life were actually made in childhood. A friend who is a poet explains why our first home, and memories of it, can be a sanctuary:

> How many times can the house of childhood be rebuilt? In my dreams it has been changed, sold to strangers, even been impossible to find, sometimes strangely relocated. Once it was found inside another house.
>
> These dreams are vivid and even now, awake, fully rational, something tells me that I might yet go back to Springs and find it – what? Changed? Simply gone? Demolished, renovated, added to?

For most of my adult life I have had this recurring dream about the house we left when I was 10 years old. I think I have had more of them in the years since our daughter was born, nearly 10 years ago.

What is this house? Is it still the ultimate sanctuary? I have lived in many beautiful places and in many old houses and owned a few ordinary suburban houses. In each – or most – of them I have sought sanctuary. For love, for study, for play, for work and hobbies, mostly for self-expression.

The idea of sanctuary as a place to go to often comes to mind. Less so, the idea of sanctuary as a place from which to emerge. Perhaps that is why my childhood home has such a presence in my dreams. It is where I came from.

DAMIAN RUTH

As a schoolgirl from the industrial city of Salford, I took any opportunity to visit remote places. I got to know the moors, and the isolated coastlines of Lancashire and Yorkshire. As a student in Edinburgh I began a life-long love affair with the Hebrides, especially the islands of Tiree, Skye and Iona. When I left Britain to travel around the world, the first place I lived was a remote island – Bermuda.

Continuing around the world, I found my way to the far north of Canada and realised the childhood dream of visiting the Arctic. For over a year I lived in Yellowknife, in the Northwest Territories, the eastern part of which is now called Nunavut. It is extremely isolated, lying 1500 kilometres north of Edmonton, the nearest city. The road link is closed twice a year: in spring, at break-up, when the ice on the Mackenzie River begins to melt and destroys the ice crossing; and in the fall, at freeze-up, when the ferry can no longer sail. In winter we were contained by dark for 19 hours a day, and could only step outside swaddled in wool and fur. Survival was a genuine issue – the temperature was extreme in winter and my memories of the pain of being out in 40 below zero are vivid. There were no trees and few plants other than the lichen that made a miniature world of colour. I can still hear the tinkling of ice breaking up, see the miracle called the Northern Lights, and remember the midnight sun. Life was timeless there in a deeper physical silence than any I have experienced since – the silence of deep snow.

The sanctuary of sacred places

The world is full of sacred places and spaces. All major spiritual traditions have many sanctuaries that are places of pilgrimage. For Christians, for instance, there is the Church of the Holy Sepulchre in Jerusalem; for Jews, the Wailing Wall in Jerusalem; for Muslims, the *Kaaba* in Mecca. In Zen Buddhist tradition it is the *Bodhgaya*, in the state of Bihar; for Hindus, the city of Varanasi; for the Shinto tradition, it is the Shrine in Ise.

What makes a place sacred? Perhaps sacred places have built up, through a history of connections, a more intense presence of spirit? I think we recognise sacredness when we are in such places. Perhaps we experience something beyond our usual sensitivities, which we cannot explain. I have known wonder in a shrine in Sri Lanka, in a Hindu temple in Calcutta, standing near the Moai of Easter Island, and at the Inca ruins of Machu Picchu in Peru. Here in New Zealand I was once taken to an ancient Māori burial site, which is wahi tapu (sacred ground), and was deeply affected by my experience there.

The sacred places that meant so much to me in Britain are still in my bones: standing stones, ancient churches, wells and crosses, shrines and priories, woods and hills, the landscape itself. Just the names of some places are enough to trigger a sense of wonder: Lindisfarne, Stonehenge, Temple Wood, Glastonbury, Lismore, Norwich, Riveaux Abbey, Pendle Hill. And most of all, the Isle of Iona.[18]

I first visited Iona briefly with my husband Doug in 2001 and there, as I entered St Columba's shrine, I had an experience that some would call a vision, others a hallucination. In the winter of 2005 I visited the island again to spend a week there alone. It was one of those intensely spiritual times. I was staying on my own in a large house on the edge of the ocean. Toward the end of the week, a hurricane devastated parts of the Inner Hebrides.[19] Ferries were cancelled, the power went off, and there was no communication between Iona and the mainland. At the height of the storm, the house was shaking in a ferocious wind – dark inside and out. Yet I felt completely safe – the entire landscape is sacred.

Isle of Iona

Hill of the Angels
Hollow of Thistles
Meadow of Lapwings
Raven's Peak
Glen of the Temple
Sacred Hollow
Cornfield of Silver
Spouting Cave
Hill of the Tongues
Weeper's Rock
Meadow of Geese
House of Peace
Height of the Tempest
Hollow of Otter
White Strand of Monks
Island of Storm[20]

My 'Iona in New Zealand' is the Southern Star Abbey, known as Kopua. The Order of Cistercians of the Strict Observance (also known as Trappists) is a Roman Catholic contemplative religious order. They follow the *Rule of Saint Benedict* – the book of precepts that informs the brotherhood – but are also guided by the *Carta Caritatis*, which was written about 1100 CE and is sometimes known as *The Rule of Love*. Everything at Kopua reflects love. That is why I could not have written this book without staying there many times over these past 10 years.

I have recuperated from illness at Kopua, made important decisions there, given my soul the space it needed, and worked on this book. Always, though, the real reason I go on a retreat is to find out what I am retreating from within myself.

Journal, May 2003, Kopua

In the abbey, a winter sun is tapping on the window. Incense melts icicles. A row of Trappist monks makes words dissolve. This is a place of mending. A place of broken bones and broken hearts. A place of love.

There is a deaf and half-blind dog eager for any pat, and a chorus of postulant birds praying outside. It's easy to imagine resurrection here, as Father John whips up the drive on his new farm bike and the hermit brings up an armful of spicy scones.

Every day, so many acts of kindness from the monks: a copy of a reading or a line of chant that I couldn't quite get, and the smiles, the willingness to listen. There are so many acts of kindness from the Companions, who support the monks in their work; and there is the kindness of strangers – other guests who accept a wish for silence or a need to talk. All the time, I am cared for physically, with meals and accommodation, and warmth, so I am simply free to be *and* become.

A long time ago, I was at a drum dance in the small settlement of Dettah, on the edge of the Great Slave Lake in Canada. The two women in the photograph belong to the Tłı̨chǫ First Nation, once known as Dogrib Indians, part of the Dene people. I love looking at this photo, remembering the kindness of strangers. Yellowknife, 1973.

love of people

The sanctuary of love

A friend once described her marriage as a sanctuary. She talked of feeling completely safe, cared for and loved. She had the freedom to be who she was and the opportunity to grow. Perhaps I remember it so well because at that time I had no such sanctuary. It was much later in my life that I found the sanctuary of love.

I mentioned earlier in the book that Doug and I lived apart for some years. However, we got back together again and resumed our marriage. Maybe the word love should be reserved until a relationship has lasted for a long time and gone through many ups and downs. Maybe love is what happens through commitment. Maybe love is what we *do* as much as what we *feel*? Maybe love is commitment itself?

Writing this book I have contemplated my marriage a great deal and see so clearly the ways in which it is a sanctuary for me. Doug is a gentle, steady, thoughtful man and he provides one of the things I most need in life – stability. He accepts things *as they are*. He once told me that our marriage is a haven because it is where he can be himself.

Five love poems[21]

In the mathematician's house

In the mathematician's house
there are formulas for everything.
For pressing silver, warmth
for light, for magic.

I pick my way across the pi-squared
charts while he brews a cup of tea
and see his double-dutch-all-greek-to-me
scribbles everywhere.

He emerges from the kitchen.
Innocence carrying a teapot
lovingly filled to the brim, and scones
precisely cut in hexagons.

The quietness of love

I told him of a kind of love called maintenance.
He gazed at me, soft-focus, behind his glasses
the way he does, and asked

'Do you mean I'm just a maintenance man?'
I fell back into silence left by closing doors
slammed shut on open hands.

I had meant a lasting love.
The sort which parks the car on icy nights
feeds the cat when I'm away, gives me time to find

that missing sentence. The kind of love
which says 'It must be Friday' when I'm sad
and laughs with me in sudden senseless joy.

This matters more to me than any full-flushed
sunrise shouting yellow at the sky.
Or paper streamers screaming love from planes.

I thought you'd understand. I think you do.
But maintenance men are often slow
to see their worth, or recognise
my love.

Tapestries

Quite late, these tapestries of ours combined.
The past, by then, already in its frame.
Quite late, these silver threads of ours entwined,
when innocence was far too old to claim.
What if we'd met when we were both still young,
before the warp and weft were firmly fixed?
What if we'd met before the loom was strung,
the pattern sketched, the colours so well mixed?
I've loved you in a thousand different shades.
I've lost you, found you, run away, run back.
If love were simple it could not persuade
such rainbows to cascade from white and black.
Our past is woven tight. The future's clear.
It's only now that matters. With you, here.

The count of everything

The way we place two white chairs on grass
facing each other, as if in conversation.
The lines of our house, the precise angle of its roof.
Morning nod. Dishevelled dressing gown.
Newspaper. Shopping list. Kettle on.
Our evening ritual: firelight, dinner, news.
The cats in front of the hearth.
You, doing equations as the night resolves itself.
Man and woman face the same conclusion.
We're as old as the grandfather clock,
as new as the second hand.
We're timeless as space between.
We stand inside this ordinary day.
Extraordinary, how the years can fall away.

How rituals are made

Asleep on Lilla's quilt of wedding rings,
a pattern bold as gold and strong as silk,
two cats curled up inside a dream of wings,
open their mouths like kittens lapping milk.
We've been ill this winter. Life too hard to alter.
Too tired to talk, too fraught for deaf and mute.
In early times this might have made love falter.
As we get old, it seems to bear new fruit.
In the dark we say goodnight by fingertip,
join hands to form a language without words.
We have to make new rituals lest love should slip.
The cats have long since freed their shadow birds.
We sleep, we dream, and somewhere in between
a world exists where words have never been.

The sanctuary of friends and family

I have always been puzzled by what family means. My only surviving family of origin is my brother and his family in England, and I have no children of my own. For a long time now, I have seen close friends as a kind of family. Later, through Doug, I acquired a large extended family: several brothers- and sisters-in-law, five stepchildren, and an ever increasing number of grandchildren and great-grandchildren. Now, I see my family as a combination of my relatives and my closest friends. Transient experiences of family are also important to me. For instance, even though I go to Kopua mainly for silence and solitude, I feel part of a family while I am there.

At home, because we love cats, even pets are part of the family.

Journal, June 2011

Last night, after dinner, we lay in front of the fire, under Lilla's quilt, warm and silent. The cats jumped up and settled down to sleep on Doug's chest. Then the four of us snoozed by candlelight and firelight, until past midnight.

What makes a friendship a sanctuary? It is somewhere we can share our deepest feelings, be heard without judgement, take risks yet be safe, be held but be free. Ideally, friends know each other as they really are and accept each other. They love, protect and treasure each other and help each other be the best they can be. And realistically, they forgive each other when the ideal is impossible!

Friendship lets you in and lets you out. It is a space of authenticity, warmth, openness, depth, closeness yet separateness. The most rewarding thing about a good friendship is being your own true self in the company of someone being *their* own true self. I love getting together with a close friend and just *being real*.

Sanctuary. It usually happens on a Tuesday evening, once a month, at the same location, a small Indian restaurant, in Raumati. We email each other to clarify the date and time. Ten minutes before the appointed time, I get in the car and head to the beach to take the Marine Parade route, catching glimpses of sea and island. Then I meander through beach suburbia, excitement growing; park in front of the restaurant, never very busy on a Tuesday.

There they are, seated across from one another, at the same table, one bottle of wine each, dressed to mark the event as special. Hello! Hello! Kiss, kiss on cheeks. Settle into chair, pour wine from my own bottle and bliss begins. My two lovely friends, Janet and Julie, a peaceful, giggle-full, sojourn into female companionship, reality, history, the three of us relishing Story.

We bring things to share – a photo, a piece of jewellery, a description of a past event – the items are agreed upon beforehand. We listen and we are heard, for real: a refuge in the Now.

Two to three hours later, bill divided: farewells. Return to the day-to-day, now nurtured and refreshed.

LESLIE CLAGUE

When I met to talk about the nature of sanctuary with another friend, Ann, who is a psychotherapist, she said she'd prefer to talk about sanctuary together, rather than write about it alone. She explained that the act of sharing ideas with others face to face was itself a sanctuary. I scribbled a few of her words down during our conversation:

> Being with people I love and trust and care about and having that interchange is one of my sanctuaries. I'm talking about words – putting out and getting back and connecting in and being part of: words and non-verbal words. I think this connection actually produces an additional energy or entity in space and time and a creative context.
>
> ANN NATION

Friendship beyond death

Some people are soul mates. I met such a friend in 1966, on our first day as students at Edinburgh University, both of us nervous about our new world of learning. Our backgrounds and lives were completely different. Betty Munnoch was Canadian by birth, now raising a large family in Scotland where she had settled with her husband Alex. She was 20 years older than I was.

After our time in Edinburgh, our friendship continued to grow despite the fact that we lived on different sides of the world. We shared a great love of literature. We were both fascinated by collecting old china and whenever I went back to Britain we would set up a stall together at an antique fair. We stayed in touch regularly by letter and phone. Most crucially, though, we stayed connected by a kind of thought transference, and often experienced synchronicities of ideas.

Betty died on Christmas Day, 2002. It was a long, slow dying: the cancer took three years. Yet we always talked of life – I have never known anyone with such a passion for life. Betty relished every detail. Her attitude to life was 'More fun!' Shortly after her death, I came across the words *anam cara*,[22] which is the old Gaelic phrase meaning soul-friend. John O'Donoghue, the Irish mystic and poet, described it: 'This friendship was an act of recognition and belonging. When you had an *anam cara*, your friendship cut across all convention and category. You were joined in an ancient and eternal way with the friend of your soul.'[23]

Some days the air is full of the spirit of my *anam cara*.

The sanctuary of strangers

Strangers have helped me many times in my life. I recall moments far away from home, being welcomed into someone else's world. Here is a friend's account of such an experience:

> I travelled to Whangarei to take up a holiday job on a farm. I arrived a day early and had only 50 cents left in my funds. Unconcerned, I went to the farm (the job included full board) to settle in ready to start work the next day. The farmer was away and the housekeeper would not allow me to stay. 'Go away, come back tomorrow.'
>
> I drove 40 miles back to Whangarei, on my scooter, to stay at the Youth Hostel, which then cost 50 cents a night. It was full and I was out of luck. So at 6.30 pm in a town where I knew no one, in midwinter, and with no money, I was in serious strife.
>
> I spent an hour feeling increasingly panic-stricken then returned to the Youth Hostel to plead my case. I explained the situation to the manager. He wasn't bothered and said there was nothing he could do. As I walked away, as an afterthought, he said, 'You could try the Andrews, sometimes they take our overflow in summer.' He gave me the address.
>
> It was a big old house with a big garden. The door was answered by an elderly lady – after 8 pm. She said, 'Come in; you must be cold.' I was welcomed as if I was a well-loved daughter. No questions, just gentle care: a fine meal, bath, comfortable bed, breakfast and lunch the following day: a gentle day, sitting in the garden, in quiet communion with my hostess.
>
> When I left, payment was refused, a gift of fruit and biscuits given for my journey, and a promise extracted to return the following Sunday – my day off – for midday dinner. The job proved to be a disaster – slave labour 12 hours a day with very basic living arrangements and food, although I was allowed free petrol from the farm tank for my scooter.
>
> Mrs Andrews gave me bed and meals every weekend – I finished work Saturday lunchtime and had Sundays off. She never accepted anything in return and never expected anything of me. She gave me sanctuary. She wrote to me for several years after I left. When I first met her she was 85.
>
> KATHY ANSIN

The sanctuary of ancestors

At Kopua, over the winter months, Father Niko keeps a huge log fire going day and night in the guesthouse. After Vigils, when it is still dark, I hunch over the fire, leaning towards the heat, warming my face, just like my dad used to do. As I sit there in firelight, I feel connected with my ancestors.

My grandmother Gertrude had a great influence on my life. She was a storyteller, with a marvellous imagination. When I remember her now, I think nothing is impossible. When Gertrude married my grandfather, who was an Irish Catholic, her family disowned her. Her father had come to England from Germany as a young man. He was a tailor, as was his father before him.

One day at school, when I was nine, I had a premonition about her death. When I went home that afternoon I found out that she had died. My grandmother's death was the most significant event of my childhood. We used to visit her grave and it was not long after this that I began to see the ghosts. But that story comes later in the book.

After my first marriage ended, I changed my surname and took my grandmother's maiden name.

Kindling

My husband says a good fire lights itself but nothing's as good as kindling, even flames. Kindling holds the secret fire of life.

I wait for the snap of autumn to crack the branches, and after each storm, forage beneath trees, collecting broken sticks to hoard in sacks and boxes. I stash them in the corner of the garage.

I used to gather kindling for my grandmother, from the giant trees that lined Oak Road. Then the council razed them and planted saplings, changing the sign to Ash Road, as if we wouldn't twig. But I am a keeper of memories; what's more, I write them down. Once there were giant oaks along that road.

Once there was a mother with her craft of kindling. Once there was a child who learnt to tie up twigs with thread. And once, there was a grandmother, huddled in her crocheted shawl, staring into the fire until she read its heart.

We gathered like witches – my mother, me, and the old one – whispering the stories we saw within. Kindling is a part of kith and kin. Kindling is a kindness in this world.

Later, I lived on the edge of the sea and gathered tinder from the beach – a kindness from Kapiti. Snaps of wood, flung up on some past high tide. Clumps of shrivelled seaweed plucked for luck. People warned that salt would rot my grate, but the sea's kindling sparked me back to life. Fires in the setting sun, fires at full moon. The fires of survival warmed me to my core. The gods of the hearth were close.

By then, my mother lived in the Ash Road house. And now, the chimney was declared unsafe. They filled the fireplace in and my mother bought an electric fire with coloured coals; concealed beneath them, a metal disk with blades rotated around red globes. She loved the glow of instant kindling – her endless setting sun.

The line of oaks finally turned to ash and my mother went into a nursing home. I asked them to let her take her instant fire. They said it wasn't possible – there were rules about safety.

I begged.

They conceded.

An electrician came to disconnect the heat and sign a certificate that said the fire was dead.

Partly, he was right. But mostly, wrong.

Doug and our granddaughter Juliette cannot have a conversation, because Doug is profoundly deaf. Yet here they are, totally absorbed in deep communication. Carterton, 2012.

freedom of mind

The sanctuary of imagination

Once, I was watching a sunrise with my granddaughter Nesta, who was about five at the time. She took hold of my hand and said, 'It's like being in a poem.'

Imagination is timeless and spaceless. Within it, we can create any time and place we want. In imagination, we can take the ingredients of existence and transform them into a perfect world. Images cascade like showers of stars on the darkest night.

As we move from being children to adults, there is a danger that the *way* we are taught to think limits us. I was mostly taught, for example, to categorise, analyse, abstract and synthesise. So I am drawn towards dichotomies and classifications rather than ambiguous possibility and blurred boundaries. Yet life has taught me that it is in uncertainty that understanding hides.

How can I break out of those old linear and circular patterns of thinking? If I am to enter the sanctuary of mind deeply I must abandon logic and certainty. How else, watching the sunrise, could Nesta have imagined she was in a poem? John Keats would have said that she was demonstrating 'negative capability', that faculty in which we are 'capable of being in uncertainties, mysteries, doubts, without any irritable reaching after fact and reason'.[24]

The world of fantasy is open to us all. We dream and we daydream. Our minds contain the power to create infinite sanctuaries where we feel treasured and safe from harm. Here is an imagined sanctuary from one of my childhood friends:

> A nice cosy lounge with a log fire, like maybe a stone fireplace with a big lintel and an iron grate and hearth with a fender. And a nice little rug in front. A couple of wooden rocking chairs. Some paraffin lamps hanging in the alcoves at the side of the fireplace.
>
> I'm sitting there listening to some music. The curtains are drawn – it's dark outside. It's winter. There's a whiff of paraffin from the lamps. Behind a rocking chair, there's a very dark oak table, with some dried flowers in a little jug. The jug is one of those ceramic ones like a fallen log and the dried flowers are sticking out from it.
>
> The table has leaves that pull out and it's well scratched from people doing things on it. On it, there's a blue willow pattern teapot waiting for someone to brew up; and a couple of cups, also waiting.
>
> In front of the crackling log fire, curled up on the old rug, and purring calmly away, is a lovely fat marmalade cat, with a brilliant white fluffy diamond on his chest.
>
> It's nice and cosy in there.

There's a kind of 1970s Sanyo music centre. It would be better if it was a gramophone. Some LPs in a little cupboard. Some Caruso. Yes, an old record player. Twenty or 30 LPs that you bought for 10 pence each in a second-hand shop. Probably the Houghton Weavers and Harry Secombe and maybe one or two comic things like the Two Ronnies.

Flock wallpaper or a little Laura Ashley print. Heavy damask curtains. Some cactus on the window ledge. Leaded glass and the top windows have flowers in them.

It's not somewhere I've lived. It's in my head. A place to go.

BARRY LENT

All my life I have preferred to give in to imagination rather than risk losing it. When I was studying psychology, in my twenties, I used to try to free the way I thought by practising creative thinking techniques.[25] But I now believe that the best way to liberate thoughts is to *suspend* thinking altogether!

We need to dream. We need to daydream. We need to be in a space which is somewhere between light and dark. We need the sanctuary of shadowland. When I am there, all my senses are as one: hearing, seeing, tasting, smelling, touching and those other senses we have but have not yet named, which for now I will call intuition.

The sanctuary of wandering

A mind needs to *wander*. It needs to amble and stare into space. A mind sometimes just wants to be a vagabond – a fetching word that comes from the late Latin *vagabundus* meaning strolling about. When I think of my vagabond mind, the pleasures it can give me (as well as the trouble it can get me into) I feel a kind of indulgent affection.

William Henry Davies was a wanderer who came to be called 'the poet of tramps'. He wrote one of most loved poems in the English language:

Leisure

What is this life if, full of care,
We have no time to stand and stare?

No time to stand beneath the boughs
And stare as long as sheep or cows.

No time to see, when woods we pass,
Where squirrels hide their nuts in grass.

No time to see, in broad daylight,
Streams full of stars, like skies at night.

No time to turn at Beauty's glance,
And watch her feet, how they can dance.

No time to wait till her mouth can
Enrich that smile her eyes began.

A poor life this if, full of care,
We have no time to stand and stare.[26]

Wandering is one of those words that compresses a double-edged concept. Teasing it apart can help us learn about our own ambivalences. We make heroes out of wanderers, explorers and seafarers. We find something enigmatic, even noble, about 'gentlemen of the road'. Yet we look down on vagrants, tramps and strays. At worst, society persecutes 'travellers' and other nomadic people. We want to explore, yet stay on the beaten track; take risks yet be safe; discover yet hold on to old ideas; be original but conform.

The sanctuary of sleep

When I began to study Judaism, I came across the belief that when we sleep our soul returns to its source. The moment I read about this, I knew it to be true. In his superb book *The River of Light: Spirituality, Judaism, consciousness,* Rabbi Lawrence Kushner explores the meaning of the Torah as if he were interpreting a dream: 'There is a realm of being that comes before us and follows after us. Streaming through and uniting all creation. Knowing who we have been and will be ... It is a river of light.'[27]

Journal, April 2011, Kopua

I can't find words for the book any more. I have to trust they will come, but why would words want to come to someone so muddled and tired and confused? Words wouldn't want to waste their time. You say this is my job. I'm supposed to do this. Show me, please show me ...

I lay my head on a fathomless pillow made from the down of a thousand white geese who have flown across the Arctic mountains, over the rim of the world and back again. I swim in time, feeling the seconds slide away from my skin.

I wake with words in my mouth and write them down, without thinking what they mean.

[days later]...

Time has ceased to matter. When? The day before yesterday? At some point ... I finished a very rough first draft. Maybe during last night or the one before last?

Journal, July 2011, Kopua

I've been struggling to write again.

Words are dust in my mouth. Chalk. Cardboard.

I've lost the connection.

Every time I get close to God, I cry. Then I pull back again. Last night I didn't hold back and cried myself to sleep.

Early this morning I woke with words in my mouth again.

Later, I stepped out into the dark to go across to the church for Vigils. The constellations are back. Intense, clear, near.

The sanctuary of dreams

It seems to be human nature to interpret the inner space of dreams. People have done so for thousands of years. Many ancient societies, religions and philosophies described dreams as communication from the spiritual world.[28]

Years ago I studied Freudian dream analysis, a formal and time-consuming technique.[29] It taught me to listen to my own intuition when interpreting a dream and that only the dream's dreamer can interpret it. Sometimes dreams can be so vivid that I am not sure what the difference is between a dream and a vision. When I was so ill, around the time I retired, I had a series of dreams about healing, all of which seemed to be saying, '*Imagine* being well and you *will* be well.'

Journal, January 2001

I got very sick when I got home from the trip up north. I had terrible pain everywhere as if all my joints were on fire and I was getting those 'electric shocks' in my head again. That night I had a dream. It was as if I was shown the way to be healed and to heal.

I must have dreamt it. I don't know. Maybe I got delirious. But something significant happened that night. In the dream, bit by bit, every single pain was eased until I seemed to be floating above the bed.

I was given a kind of message – not in words, more in concept – about what was needed for healing. It was this: there are not enough resources in the world to heal, so what we have to do is imagine what we need and that is enough. There were eight things that are needed for healing. Some I remember, others I have now forgotten. One stood out: there is just not enough blue in the world but we can make blue by 'seeing' it. That is all we have to do. Believe.

The next day I slept all day. I knew something had changed. Something had burned up and gone. Since then, I have felt an immense sense of calm – a kind of wellbeing. I have stopped struggling so much. I think God is looking after me.

Journal, February 2001

Another dream. Some kind of intergalactic event and there were eight (again eight!) 'auditors' of this event. I passed two men standing by telescopes. They were two of the auditors. I just happened to be there at the right time and I watched this event through a huge glass window. Several suns came together and merged into the most dazzling colours of sunset.

This dream moved straight into another, where people flew in the sky with their arms outstretched. They were swooping up into the sky with the most enormous sense of freedom. I just watched them but I saw that it was possible.

Even when a dream takes the form of a nightmare, it can be pointing to a way to heal. Years ago, a friend had a horrible recurring dream in which she was looking after a baby who was starving to death. No matter what she did, she couldn't feed the baby. Night after night, it was getting thinner and fading away. My friend felt as if she was being forced, in the dream, to watch the baby die.

Eventually, she saw meaning in her dream. The baby was herself. She had left no time in her life to feed her own soul. Once she began to take time to do the things her soul longed to do, the nightmare did not return.

The sanctuary of creativity

Creativity is something our soul gives us to play with when it's pleased with us. Or, something our soul gives us to struggle with when we need to find a way out of despair. We are *all* creative but often don't appreciate our creativity. We use our minds to find ways to express love, raise a family, provide food and shelter, and make our way in the world. We gather information and knowledge, experience life internally, and turn it into understanding and wisdom. We turn ideas into symbols, metaphors, allegories, parables and proverbs. We remember ideas as legends, fables, myths and stories.[30]

The mind is one of the most powerful sanctuaries we have. In the space of the mind, we can transform experience into ideas, and ideas into language, music, movement, art, mathematics, and all the other forms we have of expression. When we mind something we are *relating* to it: we think about it, long for it, pay attention to it, object or take offence to it, care about it, look after it, watch over it, remember it. I mind therefore I am.

We are our own historians as we record and interpret our story within the sanctuary of memory and, through that, we continuously revise it. In one of the most creative and moving replies to my question about sanctuary, an acquaintance who is a writer expresses the power of memory and storytelling:

> Sanctuary means a safe place. In the late 1930s there were not many safe places left in Europe. My family lived in Glasgow near the docks on the River Clyde and the docks were an obvious target for the Luftwaffe. War with Germany seemed inevitable so my parents decided that my mother, my brother and I should leave Glasgow for my mother's father's home in the Scottish Borders.
>
> I was five and my brother not quite one year old when we went to live in my grandfather's cottage. There we remained until I was 10 years old, the summer of 1944. Each year thereafter until I was 17, I, together with my brother and sister who was born in 1945, spent two summer months, the school holiday months of July and August, at my grandfather's. What began as a safe place, a sanctuary from war, became associated with leisure, pleasure and happiness. My grandfather died in 1953. His heir sold the cottage and it was lost to me for what I thought would be forever. I was wrong.
>
> In my mind, the cottage remains as it was when I was a child and a young woman. I can go back any time I want, walk in the door, go into the kitchen, sit in my grandmother's rocking chair, listen to the French gilt clock ticking away under its glass dome. I can cross the room to the chest of drawers, deep red mahogany and highly polished, open the drawers one by one each full of the treasures my grandfather collected. A good fire is burning in the range and the 'girdle' (griddle) hangs ready to be swung across the fire to bake my mother's scones and pancakes. I visit each of the downstairs rooms in turn: the scullery where I washed so many dishes, scrubbed so many pots and pans; the sitting room where no one ever sat, for they sat in the kitchen, around the table for meals or beside the fire to chat. I can go upstairs, treading the turkey-red carpet held in place by brass rods so often polished by me. There are two bedrooms, huge bedrooms, one for us and one for visitors. My grandfather had the small bedroom downstairs behind the sitting room away from the noisy children. Between the bedrooms, at the head of the stairs, is the 'linkey hole' (cupboard). Everything is in the linkey hole, our books – and what books there were, for my grandfather went to every house sale in the shire. What better to do on a wet day than to lisp my way through a Spanish primer or to peruse a weighty tome on how to manage a Victorian household?
>
> There have been times in my life when I felt alone, afraid, and even desperate. Nights when I lay sleepless, needing someone, needing

something, needing somewhere, needing sanctuary. I could always find sanctuary if I closed my eyes and opened my mind.

What is time? We measure it: seconds, minutes, hours, days, weeks, months, years, centuries. Or is time like leaves in a calendar? Leaves we can riffle backwards and forwards at will? Do I reach back through some ripples in time to find my sanctuary? Am I actually there, and, if so, in what shape and form? Does my child self haunt my grandfather's cottage? I think what I have been trying to say is that there are no longer any physical sanctuaries in the modern world. We have to create our own by whatever means we can. Many people go on retreats, divorce themselves from the harsh realities of modern living. The result may be spiritual cleansing but how long does it last once they return to their daily lives? I believe that sanctuary lies within every one of us, as we ought to be able to reach it without hiding away from life.

MARY SIMONS

The sanctuary of remembering

Memory is Aladdin's lamp. We can have almost anything we wish from the past, just by polishing it up – or not. We can preserve, forget or alter as we reflect on the totality of the past. We try to make sense of it, learn from it, and integrate our self on a continuum of time.

Memory is not mere storage, it is synthesis, transformation. We *change* our memories over time. We can nurture memory, by making notes, taking photographs, keeping a journal or by verbalising an experience. The key to remembering is paying attention.

I have always been interested in memory: from a childhood listening to my grandparents' stories of the past, right through to adulthood and my choice of memory as the subject for my doctoral thesis.

In the 1960s, Russian neuropsychologist Alexsandr Luria wrote two compelling case studies. They were the first books I ever read on memory … and to this day I still think they are the most fascinating. *The Mind of a Mnemonist* was about a man, called 'S', who could not forget anything.[31] He was so overwhelmed by detail that he was unable to focus on anything real. 'Indeed,' said Luria, 'one would be hard put to say which was more real for him: the world of imagination in which he lived or the world of reality in which he was but a temporary guest.'[32] *The Man with a Shattered World* was about a soldier called Zasetsky, who had a brain injury that meant he no longer had a functioning memory.[33] He had immense difficulty following simple directions and lived in a state of emotional and psychological disarray. I wonder, which would be worse – all or nothing?

When I was told I might be losing my memory, I began a project to remember, or rather, to reconstruct, as much about my life as possible. I began very simply by taking a blank page for each year of my life and writing down where I had lived and who had been present in my life at that time. I have kept a diary since I was seven and that made it easier, as did the collections of photographs I have gathered during my life. Gradually, I included important events, then descriptions of people and places, then anecdotes. I began to re-member myself – put myself together again.

My memory became a sanctuary where I began to heal. I *consciously* reintegrated myself across my whole life and I felt whole again. It rekindled my sense of belonging, meaning and love. I gathered myself up in my own arms. I also realised that time and again I had repeated certain patterns of behaviour and I began to understand the structure of my life.

This project showed me the phenomenal power of memory. Memory holds the key to being alive *now*. We can remember or forget and that means we can control our *relationship* with time. Memory shapes the nature of our existence. Without memory, do we even exist?

John O'Donohue called memory 'an invisible sanctuary':

> There is a harvesting imagination that works at the heart of memory, which searches the lived substance of our days, until it clarifies and settles into a form that abides. Almost without our noticing it, the individual sanctuary of memory is forever finding its way into further structure and shape. This work continues until the substance of our last hours on earth is received into its deeper, lived form. When at last the body falls and the visible life vanishes, the finished sanctuary of memory holds all the harvested possibility.[34]

Memory means we can enter a sanctuary again and again, simply by remembering a *previous* experience of sanctuary. Until a few years ago, my sister-in-law Lilla Harvie loved gardening, was an excellent pianist, baked delicious bread, turned houses into homes, and made gorgeous patchwork quilts by hand. Then she developed Parkinson's disease and gradually lost the kind of life she once had. Yet through memory, she still finds some sanctuary:

> Sanctuary to me now is sanity! And music, theatre and the arts, all brought to me on the Arts Channel. I've lost all the other things I used to do but I rediscovered music. I also have my memory of the time I spent in an ashram, in Ganeshpuri, with Guru Maya. The beauty of the place and the lovely chanting will always be there, within. It was a place of safety and sanctuary, and I can still go there in my head.
>
> LILLA HARVIE

The sanctuary of forgetting

Just as we have a sanctuary of memory, sometimes we can have the sanctuary of forgetting, creating oblivion for unbearably painful things. I say 'sometimes' because I think there are things in all our lives that are so painful we cannot forget them. All we can hope for then is to accept and forgive – ourselves and others.

I do not remember and cannot reconstruct almost a year of my life: the year before the time I was in a psychiatric hospital. Maybe the retrograde amnesia is due to the excessive antipsychotic medication that was sometimes forced down me, but I also made a *decision* to forget. When I left hospital, I burnt journals, poems and letters from that time – even a manuscript for a book. In return, I was given the gift of forgetting. My past is undoubtedly still part of me but I can no longer relive in my mind the details of that time. However, I think the body holds memories we cannot erase.

Some years later, I again used the mind's capacity to forget. In my studio there is a large old-fashioned trunk that came from England to New Zealand, with all my possessions. Over the years I have used it use it to store important letters, documents and mementos. One winter, extremely depressed, I went through the trunk and threw out anything at all that reminded me of the sorrows in my life. I *consciously* sifted through my past as my mind made it mine to remember, or not.

We are the chief curators of our own past: to remember it *as we will*. We shape our memory, consciously or not. We unconsciously remember some things and forget others. We also *choose* to remember some things and to forget others. We construct our own 'truth'. This is what makes memory a sanctuary – as long as it is intact.

In *The Celtic Twilight: Myth, fantasy and folklore*, Irish poet W.B. Yeats describes the process:

> The things a man has heard and seen are threads of life; and if he pull them carefully from the confused distaff of memory, any who will can weave them into whatever garments of belief please them best. I too have woven my garment like another, but I shall try to keep warm in it, and shall be well content if it do not unbecome me.[35]

The sanctuary of reading …

In his autobiography, Bertrand Russell writes to a friend:

> A life in books has great calm and peace … I am constructing a mental cloister, in which my inner soul is to dwell in peace, while an outer simulacrum goes out to meet the world. In this inner sanctuary I sit and think spectral thoughts. Yesterday, talking on the terrace, the ghosts of all former occasions there rose, and walked

> before me in solemn procession – all dead, with their hopes and fears, their joys and sorrows, their aspirations and their golden youth – gone, gone into the great limbo of human folly. And as I talked, I felt myself and the others already faded into the past, and all seemed very small; struggles, pains, everything, mere fatuity, noise and fury signifying nothing. And so calm is achieved and Fate's thunders become mere nursery talks to frighten children.[36]

... and imaginary friends

I wonder why children are allowed to have 'imaginary friends' and talk to them whereas adults are not? I only have to think of the books that have changed my life to name my own imaginary companions.

Journal, December 2008

This morning I cried when I read about Harold Pinter's death. Of course I didn't know him, but I felt that I did. Deep down, I knew Harold Pinter. He was part of my inner world from the first time I read him, when I was 16. I always felt he was a friend who understood me.

Alan Bennett is another of my imaginary friends and I wonder if he has imaginary friends too. In his play *The History Boys*, Hector the history teacher says the best moments in reading are when you come across something you thought you were the only person to think, or feel.

> Now here it is, set down by someone else, a person you have never met, someone even who is long dead. And it is as if a hand had come out and taken yours.[37]

My greatest love in literature is poetry, a love nurtured by my mother. There are many poets whose company I keep and some of them feel like friends – Donne, Neruda, Stevens, Shakespeare, Sturm, Leunig, Dickinson, Harrison, Angelou, Stafford, Fenton, Duffy, Frost, Turner, Hughes.

Recently, I was re-reading Walter Greenwood's book about the County of Lancashire and felt a great closeness to this man who has written with such depth of love for the people of my home town. I never knew Walter, although Mum once told us that he worked alongside my grandfather Fred Halstead, in Salford, in the 1930s. This small, insignificant fact seemed important to me as I was soaking up what he had to say about Manchester in the 1940s. Then I got to the last page and Walter's hand came out from the book and took hold of mine:

> This is goodbye. I do not know about other writers, but for me I am conscious of those who

read my words, even though I do not know who they are. Writers write alone and readers read alone and so we share one thing in common – a bond of solitude.[38]

The sanctuary of writing

Writing is a solitary act that may never become an act of connection with others, yet there is still a feeling of connection in the act of writing, which goes beyond connection with oneself. I have been alone with this book for a long time now without knowing whether it will be published, yet I have a sense of closeness to some reader, in the shadows of imagination.

A word

A word is dead
When it is said,
Some say.

I say it just
Begins to live
That day.

EMILY DICKINSON[39]

The empty page is an open, receptive companion. The page and I sit in silence together and face the danger of words – the emotions they evoke, the ideas they summon, ungoverned. Writing poetry, I am on the threshold between silence and words, listening and receiving. I do not enter poetry. Poetry enters me.

I love playing with words and disappearing into alphabets, dictionaries, thesauruses, etymologies, books on synonyms, idioms, phrase and fable. My heroes: Roget, Brewer, Murray, Partridge, Fowler.[40]

We fling a string of words, like a suspension bridge, across a fast-flowing river. To meet *anywhere* on the bridge may be better than not crossing the river at all. But sometimes I wonder if our reliance on words prevents us looking for other ways to cross the river? Words are, after all, merely containers into which we try to squash experience. If we don't have a word for something, we tend to think it doesn't exist, but we just haven't named it yet. (In fact, we even have various containers, such as *ineffable,* to explain that state.)

Words slide sideways when we find it hard to communicate about some of the most intimate things about being human. We use words to camouflage the fear of uncertainty. Take death, for instance. People pass, pass over, cross over, move over, go to sleep, go on ahead, are taken, bite the dust, breathe their last, are called home, come to an end, depart, feel no pain, give up the ghost, are snuffed out, go to meet their maker, are in a better place, join the invisible choir, meet their end, pass away, slip away quietly or are with the angels. In Lancashire, they pop their clogs.

Fifty years ago, the French poet Raymond Queneau published a book of 10 sonnets in such a way that any line of any sonnet could be replaced by the equivalent in one of the remaining nine sonnets. This way he presented 10^{14} (which is 100,000,000,000,000) poems.[41]

Even more astonishing, each of those 10^{14} sonnets would, I believe, have a unique meaning for each person who read it. Each of us has a unique world of words: every word that we know has some association for us. It is astonishing that human beings can share meanings through words at all. And yet, we do.

An old friend that I haven't seen since we left school materialised in my kitchen the other day, as I opened her letter answering my question about sanctuary:

Soft and squishy duvet.

A reassuring cuddle on the sofa.

Never hearing an angry cry again.

Cooking in my kitchen.

Treading softly in my church.

Under a Lakeland summer sky.

Arriving home after a motorway trek.

Remembering fondly times from my past.

Young voices singing.

CHRISSIE JONES

The sanctuary of music

I was brought up on music. Our childhood home was full of the swinging dance music of the 1930s and 40s – my mother and father were amateur ballroom dancers. My brother is a musician who ushered me into the world of classical music. I have found sanctuary in music all my life. Sometimes music permeates my body, as though I were listening to it, not with my ears, but through the centre of my being.

In the book based on his 2006 BBC Reith Lectures, Daniel Barenboim opens the first chapter with this sentence: 'I firmly believe that it is impossible to speak about music.'[42] What I think he means, though I am not sure, is that we can only talk about our *reaction* to music. Maybe that is enough?

The sanctuary of art

Ever since I got a Box Brownie for my tenth birthday I have taken photographs, and I still find a sense of sanctuary through looking at the world through the eye of my camera. Intense, absorbed, I lose myself in something beyond myself. But I know how limited I am in appreciating paintings. I have a small attic window in my mind, through which I see one or two stars in the night sky, but I know others see the heavens.

Flung into Another Place, Bob Kerr. Oil on board, 34 x 24 cm.

Some years ago, I visited the Hermitage in St Petersburg with a colleague. As we went around, she talked about some Picassos in a way I had not heard anyone talk about art before. Later I returned to the room and looked at them again. I was certain that someone had changed the paintings. Artists whose paintings always pull me in are L.S. Lowry, J.M.W. Turner, Marc Chagall, Vincent Van Gogh, Henri Rousseau, Frida Kahlo, Rita Angus and Alfred Wallis.

A year or two ago my friend Bob Kerr gave me one of his paintings, which was titled with the first line of one of my poems. Later, when I posed my question about the meaning of sanctuary, his response was simply to ask me what I saw in the painting.

Sanctuary, Dave McCann. Ceramic with raku glaze, 26 cm high.

Someone told me of a sculptor who often visits Kopua, and who had made a sculpture called *Sanctuary*. When I finally met Dave McCann I asked him to tell me about the sculpture.

The understanding of Sanctuary as a place of personal security has left me. The understanding is groaning and growing, as the word becomes an adjective describing an indwelling knowing. The ancient psalm firstly assures me of the un-nameable God's strength and concern for me, then invites me to be still and know. Suddenly in this stillness I know this presence in me. I become living Sanctuary.

Art happens for me as a 3D manifestation of this Sanctuary when my heart and mind simply cannot contain the giftedness of the stillness. Once, as an adult student at a Māori art school, I was totally absorbed in doing an assignment while surrounded by several very spiritually open and talented fellow students. As we worked we sang a mōteatea (Māori song) together, taking turns to lead and harmonise. Our task was to design and make a figurine of a kuia, capturing the essence of what she is to the spirituality of the marae. (Anyone unfamiliar with 'kuia' could think Crone or Squaw or the Jungian description of the 'Wild woman' archetype.)

I looked up and saw through the glass panels in the door of the room a fellow female student talking to our tutor in the corridor. The two women, one old, one young, were sharing good news in a manner that only free women can. I could not hear a word that been said but I just knew young Jen was sharing the good news that she was at last pregnant to her man. 'Sanctuary' happened. There was nothing between mind and fingers. To this day I have not been able to repeat some of the technical aspects of the resultant figurine but that same knowing is alive for me.

DAVE McCANN

The sanctuary of numbers

There are innumerable other routes into the sanctuary of the mind through arts and sciences of which I have little experience, but before I leave this chapter I want to point to the path called mathematics, because I believe that Doug has experienced a kind of sanctuary there all his life: a space of intense beauty and fascination. I have observed him become so absorbed by a question that he seems to live for weeks at a time within the question itself.

Sometimes I get a hint of what might be there, in that sanctuary, when I browse through some of his books. There is this treasure for instance: *Imagining Numbers (particularly the square root of minus fifteen)* by Barry Mazur, which tells me that Girolamo Cardano was a sixteenth-century mathematician 'who invoked and used imaginary numbers like the square root of minus one'. The treatise *Ars Magna* (The Great Art), published in 1545, stands as Cardano's most influential achievement. Here is a translation of the title page:

THE GREAT ART

Or

THE RULES OF ALGEBRA

By Girolamo Cardano

Outstanding Mathematician, Philosopher and Physician

In One Book … Which is called the Perfect Work

Cardano went on to say in his first chapter: 'Since this art surpasses all human subtlety and the perspicuity of mortal talent and is a truly celestial gift and a very clear test of the capacity of men's minds, whoever applies himself to it will believe there is nothing that he cannot understand.'[43]

Children rush down into the sea after school, full of the joy of life. Raumati, 2008.

presence of body

Re-membering our body

Why did only one person who replied to me mention their body explicitly as a sanctuary? Is it because the mind, body and spirit are not separate at all and so to tease them apart to talk about them is, in a way, artificial? I only have to think of listening to music to realise that my body is as much a sanctuary as my mind and spirit, but when I began this contemplation on sanctuary, it never even occurred to me. Why was it so late in my contemplation that I came to reflect on the body as a sanctuary?

Contemplation brings awareness, which sometimes brings us face to face with difficult things in our life. Our body – its shape, size, colour, abilities, health – is permanently on view in a world that sets arbitrary standards of perfection and engages in criticism of anything less than 'perfect'. I know how easy it is to absorb and internalise such criticism, and even to disconnect from one's own body. In such circumstances it can be difficult to see the body as a sanctuary.

I have struggled with my weight all my life. Bullied at primary school, I escaped from my body into my mind. In a sense I made my mind a sanctuary for my body rather than the other way around. As the contemplation deepened, I peeled back other layers of pain, including a sexual assault by a male nurse when I was a patient in a psychiatric hospital. And so the contemplation continued until feelings that I might not otherwise have discovered emerged and were released. This is one of the rewards of contemplation: even if painful, it is *freeing*.

The joy of being

I hug my husband, make love, hold a grandchild in my arms, comfort and am comforted by touch. I sing, dance, laugh, write poetry, walk on my beloved beach, play the piano, take photographs of seagulls, get covered with paint, wander into pharmacies just to smell the perfumes, fill our pantry with bottled fruit from the garden, plant bluebells, stroke the cats, go for long walks in the rain. This is what sanctuary of the body means to me. I experience the pleasures of being alive that come from *savouring* life. The word savour is delicious: it comes from Latin *sapere*, which has two intriguingly linked meanings – to taste and to be wise. If I can't *savour* life, how can life *save* me?

Slowly, I saw that others had indeed mentioned their body as a sanctuary, but like me, they had done so obliquely: walking in the bush, swimming in the sea, listening to waves, running on a beach, gazing at the constellations, inhaling the perfumes of a garden, sharing a delicious meal with family, snuggling down into bed, nuzzling into a pet, smelling freshly baked bread, playing a game of golf, driving along in an old house bus, performing beautiful music, feeling the wind on skin, reading a treasured book, making a sculpture, being wrapped in someone's arms.

I talked to a friend about my difficulty writing this chapter, as we were swimming in the summer sea. I had previously mentioned the content of later chapters, which all have concepts beginning with S – solitude, silence, stillness, simplicity, slowness and space. The next day, she tucked a note under my windscreen wiper: 'Thank you so much for activating S activity today. S stands for Swim, Splash, Salt detox, Survive, and Spirits revived.'

My friend Myra, a writer living in London, describes a delightful experience she shared as a birthday treat:

> The Sanctuary is the name of a rather exclusive health/spa centre in Covent Garden. I was given a day at The Sanctuary for my birthday a few years ago with the promise that the giver would come with me as it is no fun on your own. Not really the spirit of true Sanctuary perhaps but for me it was wonderful.
>
> We spent the day together in luxurious white towelling bathrobes, being thoroughly pampered while we knew that all our friends and colleagues were slogging their way through their usual boring work routine. We went to relaxation sessions in rooms with a specially created ambience. When we were too hot we would swim a few leisurely strokes in the most unusually shaped pool with a Tarzan-type swing. When we were too cold we could warm up in the steam room or the sauna. When we were just right we could lie about on a lounger in any of the plant-populated areas watching carp swimming, or we could read, drink wine, eat their beautifully prepared food or do whatever else took our fancy. We spent the day, my friend and I, in a bubble for two.
>
> MYRA KERSNER

Sanctuary of breath

A year or two ago I attended a workshop called Sacred Voices, run by Cantor Robert Esformes, and saw, in a new way, the apparently simple act of breathing.[44] When we breathe, each breath has *four* stages to it, not *two* – in and out – as we usually think. We inhale, hold the presence of breath, exhale, and hold the absence of breath. You may have already discovered this, but if not, just for a moment, focus on your breathing. Pay close attention to what is going on. Keep breathing until you are aware of four stages, rather than two. Did you *notice* anything about breath entering your body?

If you are willing, do this again, more slowly. Now, as you breathe, be aware of the four stages of breathing as inspiration, fullness, expression and emptiness. Keep doing this for quite a while and ask yourself this question: Do I *take* breath or *receive* breath?

Sanctuary of singing

Is singing the purest way we can express the breath that inspires us? One of the most direct ways I nourish my soul is by singing. At Kopua, I love chanting psalms with the monks. It brings me such a sense of … what is the word? … compassion … love … relief … release. Rebbe Schneur Zalman of Liadi said, 'The tongue is the pen of the heart, but melody is the quill of the soul.'[45]

Nigunim are Jewish melodies, often without words. They were a development of the eighteenth-century Chassidic revival movement. They are haunting tunes that are often simple and are repeated until there is an outpouring of the soul. Some are laments, other extremely joyful. Novelist Elie Wiesel said: 'Their eyes closed, they sing as only Chasidim can. Ten times, fifty times, they repeat the same words, the same tune, and the song bursts their chests and lights a thousand flames in their eyes before rising higher and higher, up to the seventh heaven, if not higher, to the "Heichel hanegina," source and sanctuary of all songs.'[46]

Jill Purce, who founded an international movement to promote healing by sound, says that chanting is one of the earliest kinds of singing and one of the most primitive expressions of the soul:

> The *very act* of chanting resonates within the body itself, so that the external sound and internal experience become one and the same. Chanting brings about a state of calm and clarity, a sense of peace, quiet and relaxation, a reduction of pain in the body, a sense of order in everyday life. It is the healing and transformative power of sound that we need to explore.[47]

At the University of York, Professor David Howard is studying those extraordinary experiences we can have when listening to the pure voice of a child chorister. He is examining changes in the sound frequencies at the exact moment the listener feels uplifted by the music:

> In our experiments it looks as if that particular 'ring' is happening above the normal speech area, in the region up around 8,000 Hz, where there is something appearing when you get this really shimmery sound … It's something that makes you sit up, it's something that communicates with the soul. It's way beyond the words, it's way beyond the music, it's something about the content going from the brain of a singer to the brain of a listener.[48]

Sanctuary of dance

You might say I was brought up on the delight of dance. Earlier, I mentioned that my parents loved dancing. My mother had style and my father had rhythm. I remember taking ballroom classes as a young girl; and then came the magic moment when my dad took my hand and led me onto the floor at the Blackpool Tower Ballroom to swirl into one of my best memories.

As a child I also delighted in spinning around until I was dizzy. Even as an adult, I enjoy spinning around in the sea until I feel dizzy. It is a strange behaviour I suppose but what I discovered a long time ago was that my mind then becomes a still point. It gives me the tiniest glimpse into the world of the whirling dervishes, members of a Sufi order who carry on the mystical traditions of Islam. David Cooper explains that the Sufis repeat a *dhikr* (mantra) as they spin while 'whirling the head in a characteristic circular motion ... This action may be repeated hundreds, even thousands of times ... Whirling dervishes add another dimension to their practice. Whereas the *dhikr* described above is usually performed seated, either alone or in a circle of fellow participants, the whirling dervishes stand and twirl their entire bodies.'[49]

For the Dene people of Canada, dancing is 'a part of a spiritual belief Dene Elders have repeated in myths, legends, songs, and stories to young children. The Elders know that the heartbeat of song, dance and the Spirit of the drum are in the soul of each child. The Dene say that the child is born with a drum in its hand.'[50] At Dettah, near Yellowknife, I once watched a drum dance and then was invited to join in. Later in the tiny settlement of Kuglukluk, on the edge of the Arctic Ocean, I was given the same joy, at an Inuit drum dance. Dancing is *being*.

In summer, I walk along the beach with bare feet, at the edge of the waves, feeling the water on the soles of my feet. Sometimes, when I'm lucky, there is a light rain. On such a morning, with the sea water under my feet and sky water over my head, I become rain. At some point during the walk, I stand in the waves, looking out to the ocean, and listen to a particular piece of music. Then I slowly move my body until I feel part of ocean and sky. I am a human *being*.

Sanctuary of walking

Thursday 4th

Been on a long walk north
to the edge of ice
and melt in the mouth conclusions.

Thursday 11th

Water leaves its mark.
When I hold myself up
to light I can see my heart.

Thursday 18th

We wheel around like gulls,
repeating our lives again and again.
Creatures of the magnetic circle.

Sunday 21st

When I think about things
I get tangled in seaweed.
When I walk into water
Everything's clear.

Wednesday 31st

Small bones on the beach
washed white by salt
tell me life is the poem.

EXTRACTS FROM 'A BEACH DIARY'[51]

Sanctuary of rest

It staggers me that, at times, I can still ignore the importance of rest and sleep. Sometimes I get so involved in something, I run out of candles to burn at both ends. Then, when ill or depressed, the penny drops, too late, that I have not been getting enough rest and that is why I am ill.

There are also endless social expectations to be busy. Why is *not* doing something never considered to be as important as doing something? Why can't we just stop for a while? Why do I sometimes feel guilty if I have a day in bed when I am not ill but just wanting a rest? Why does it seem vaguely wasteful if it's a bright sunny day and I don't want to be out there 'doing things' but just to stay inside, puddling around?

It is very difficult to *not do*. The very act of *not doing* is *a doing*. People talk all the time about what they have done but there is no way of talking about *not doing* and so it becomes a kind of covert behaviour that is faintly shameful or funny: 'taking a mental health day', 'having a duvet day', pottering, puddling, blobbing. It is socially desirable to have a holiday overseas but questionable to have one at home, underseas.

Being in the warmth of bed is one of the most healing, comforting things I know. Snuggling under a counterpane counters pain. A writer called Sark understands the value of a cosy bed:

> I fold into my mattress sometimes, a dive from some great height, a disappearance from worldly matters. I do a lot of healing in bed and in dreams. Beds are our adult cradles. We need soft respite from our stumbling and striving. A bed is a sacred land, a sheltered territory, and a place to rebuild ourselves.[52]

Sanctuary of touch

Touch is the first thing we experience. That may be why it is the most primitive and, I believe, the most powerful of all healing practices. As someone who has trouble quietening the mind, and reducing anxiety, I find touch essential. Sometimes, when Doug holds me, I almost see the electricity discharge itself as he earths me.

A former colleague said:

When we are children, we feel safe and protected in the arms of those who care for us, particularly mothers and fathers. I doubt that changes much over time and I suspect that if we are enwrapped in the arms of someone who truly cares for us, or who loves us, that is a sublime sanctuary.

DAVID CURRY

Sanctuary of making love

Making love is the most meaningful shared sanctuary I know, and, at its most intimate, the most sacred. Together, two people are held and released, given and taken. And, sometimes, a new life is created.

More poems are written about love and making love than any other topic. Here is one by one of the greatest love poets of all.

The Good-Morrow

I wonder by my troth, what thou, and I
Did, till we lov'd? were we not wean'd till then?
But suck'd on countrey pleasures, childishly?
Or snorted we in the seaven sleepers den?
T'was so; But this, all pleasures fancies bee.
If ever any beauty I did see,
Which I desir'd, and got, 'twas but a dreame of thee.

And now good morrow to our waking soules,
Which watch not one another out of feare;
For love, all love of other sights controules,
And makes one little roome, an every where.
Let sea-discoverers to new worlds have gone,
Let Maps to other, worlds on worlds have showne,
Let us possesse one world; each hath one, and is one.

My face in thine eye, thine in mine appeares,
And true plaine hearts doe in the faces rest,
Where can we finde two better hemispheares
Without sharpe North, without declining West?
What ever dyes, was not mixed equally;
If our two loves be one, or, thou and I
Love so alike, that none doe slacken, none can die.

JOHN DONNE[53]

The Song of Songs is an intimate, yearning, explicit, erotic love poem. It is commonly given a spiritual interpretation. In Judaism it is interpreted as an allegory of love between God the husband and the people of Israel, the wife. In Christianity it is seen as an allegory of the love between Christ the husband and the Church or the individual believer, as the wife. In Islam, in the Sufi tradition, it is also seen as an allegorical description of divine love.[54]

The body as sanctuary for the spirit

All major spiritual traditions see the body as a sanctuary for the spirit. Judaism and Christianity explicitly describe it as a temple for God.[55] Numerous rituals exist to purify the body and make it a strong and healthy sanctuary for the spirit.

The traditions range from the washing of hands to the use of special baths such as the *mikveh* (ritual bath) in Jewish tradition, and the Font in Christian tradition. There are dietary requirements, such as eating or not eating certain foods, or eating certain foods on specific occasions. There are physical exercises such as yoga, Tai Chi, Qigong, and there is decoration of the body, such as the *tilaka* (the forehead mark made with coloured earths in Hindu tradition). Birth rituals celebrate new life; coming of age rituals recognise that the child's body is now able to provide sanctuary for another life; marriage celebrates a sanctuary for a spiritual union through the joining of bodies; funerals return the body to fire, earth, water or air when the spirit no longer needs a physical sanctuary.

Sanctuary of death

There is a tradition among Zen monks to write a *jisei* or 'death poem' in the last moments of death. Here is an example by Gesshu Soko, who died on 10 January 1696, aged 79:

Inhale, exhale
Forward, back
Living, dying:
Arrows, let flown each to each
Meet midway and slice
The void in aimless flight –
Thus I return to the source.

And one by Hosshin, who in the thirteenth century wrote:

Coming, all is clear, no
doubt about it. Going, all is
clear, without a doubt.
What, then, is all?

The one I love most is by Shisui, who died on 9 September 1769, aged 49. 'During his last moment, Shisui's disciples requested that he write a death poem. He grasped his brush, painted a circle, cast the brush aside, and died.'[56]

essence of spirit

Southern Star Monastery one morning just after Vigils, before the lights were turned off inside the church. Kopua, 2011.

Soul, spirit and self

I make a distinction between the soul, spirit and self but if challenged could neither explain nor defend it. I *sense* that my soul is my essence. It is concealed: I cannot see, taste, hear, touch or smell it. Yet it is here. It is what I am. Sometimes I think of it as 'the space within the heart'. It's where I belong.

What then is this life force that I call the spirit? For me, it is energy coming from God whom I believe created me for a purpose. Some have no belief in a presence called God, yet still have a deep spiritual life. Others believe in many gods or many spirits or simply in the power of being human. Some of us have visions that seem spiritual and which we believe to be supernatural; some say that such experiences are within the normal range of consciousness. Spiritual beliefs are beyond explanation. They live in actions.

And what of the self? I see my self as the sum of my genetic inheritance and worldly experience. I *sense* that when I am in sanctuary, my self is listening to what the spirit is murmuring to my soul.

The gulls

How can I say what happened on that night
in the undulating silk we call the sea,
when a mist concealed the island from my sight
as I became the water; and it, me.
The gulls, that night, the gulls they came in crowds
and I was just a wave so far from shore.
I raised my arms, ready to fly through clouds,
certain they would lift me – I would soar.
There are no words to talk about such times.
No metaphors can make that world unfold
in which the universe itself is just a rhyme
and life, the rhythm death cannot withhold.
I cannot tell you when I came to earth.
I can only say it was a kind of birth.[57]

Spirit and science

In the BBC Reith Lectures in 2003, V.S. Ramachandran took listeners on an enthralling journey through the relatively new discipline of neuroscience. The subsequent book explains his prediction that it is simply a matter of time until psychiatry becomes a branch of neurology. Yet he also sees neuroscience as a philosophy and explains his own philosophical position about consciousness:

> [It] accords with the view proposed by the first Reith lecturer, Bertrand Russell, that there is no separate 'mind stuff' and 'physical stuff' in the universe: the two are one and the same.[58]

Out of the window could have flown so many things that had been part of the fabric of my intellectual life for so long. There go Freud and Jung, with Koestler hanging on to their coat-tails. And whoops! Is that the subconscious floating by on a broomstick? What now for the search for self? No need for that any more – just get a high-tech scan. What need for mystery and meaning? There isn't any! What now for spiritual beliefs? What now for God?

Eight years later, I open Ramachandran's latest book with great excitement. There it is – in the first paragraph – one of the crucial questions in any quest to understand what it is to be human: 'How can we account for all of those mysterious faculties that are so quintessentially human, such as art, language, metaphor, creativity, self awareness, and even religious sensibilities?'[59]

In *The Tell-Tale Brain: Unlocking the mystery of human nature* he explores the nature of self-awareness in greater depth, taking me on an absorbing guided tour of the wonders of the human brain. One of the main themes is: 'how your inner self interacts with the world (including the social world) while at the same time maintaining its privacy'.[60] This enigma is at the heart of my contemplation of sanctuary.

Ramachandran believes that this is a *scientific* rather than a *spiritual* question and that some time this century science will finally confront 'one of its last great mysteries, the nature of self'. So this superb scientist, whose work I deeply respect, is saying to me, your questions are not about the spirit at all. They are about the brain and how it works.

And then I come to the final paragraph in his book. What does he do? The scientist becomes a poet!

> Across vast stretches of inhospitable space and immeasurable time, there suddenly emerged a person called Me or I. Where does this person come from? Why here? Why now? You who are made of stardust, are now standing on a cliff, gazing at the starlit sky pondering your own origins and your place in the cosmos. Perhaps another human being stood in that very same spot fifty thousand years ago, asking the very same question.[61]

I have no doubt that Ramanchadran's scientific analysis is inspired, but neither do I doubt my spiritual beliefs. So, where does that leave me? Would it matter if Ramachandran were to find God in a neurone? I know God is there anyway; I just don't position God so precisely.

Because something is *physical*, does that make it any less *spiritual*? Because something is *spiritual*, does it make it any less *physical*?

Journal, February 2006

Today, the beach knows something I don't.
Hunchback gulls stalk a quiver of terns.

Tiny fish, like tokens, stick to the littoral. People turn back, yet can't say why.

A blind man is etching symbols in the sand.
With his white cane, he pushes the driftwood aside, as if it did something wrong by coming in.

Maybe he can see much more than we can.

I've heard several accounts of spiritual experiences that people have seen as sanctuary. Some of these were triggered by a crisis, others seemed to be an unexpected gift. Here are two from completely different perspectives. The first is from a cranial osteopath who trained in medicine:

> An experience 18 years ago has remained pivotal in my life. I was invited to travel to Kapiti Island with friends and we walked into the valley at the northern end of the island. It was a beautiful sunny day. We walked for perhaps 20 minutes when I noted ahead a perfect circle of green ferns that seemed to vibrate with new energy and life. We carefully entered the circle and placed ourselves in an easy wide triangle and settled in for some quiet time to meditate. After only a few centring breaths my own personal peak experience arrived in the form of six beings of white light standing around the inner circle. Each of these angels or beings spoke to me in an energy-based or vibrational way that seemed to relate to my chakra system. Beginning with the base chakra, the being that 'spoke' to me drew me into a vision of being part of Kapiti Island.
>
> I lost my personal boundaries of body and felt myself become one with the island. I could feel the waves lapping at the edges of my awareness and see/feel the manta rays swimming in the shallows. Each of these light beings in turn spent a few moments communing with me and yet I felt enormous amounts of information flowing to me. It is not so important to recall or try to recount what each message was but to remember the sense of belonging and oneness that enveloped me with this family of light beings.
>
> The final energy that spoke to me showed me powerful images that more closely resembled speech and thought processes in my mind. I was filled with a bliss that it seems totally inadequate to try to describe with words. It was now time for them to leave and I wanted nothing more than to leave my body behind and travel with them. My sixth chakra 'angel' friend explained that they would not come to me again in this way as it was too hard on my

incarnate spirit but that they would be with me and waiting for me when I finished my current work in this body. These six were somehow part of my spirit family and they came to remind me of that fact.

I came back to myself and was crying, simply for the loss of the spiritual feeling of belonging. My friends comforted me and let me cry until I was able to tell them I was all right and simply happy.

I struggled briefly to find a place for this experience. Being trained in medicine I knew 'professionals' would place this firmly in the arena of 'delusions of grandeur' but the feeling was so personal and so powerful that I quickly released that judgement of myself and was simply thankful to have had the experience. I did travel back to this spot on two later occasions and had restful and invigorating meditation time, but no return of my Light Family.

ELAINE YOUNGS

The second example of sanctuary is rather unusual because it comes from a stranger. I had a strong intuition to ask this person, who turned out to be a farmer, if the word sanctuary meant anything to him. He told me this story:

I had a terrible accident and ended up trapped underneath my four-wheel motorbike on the farm. I'd broken my back in four places and was crushed under the weight of the bike. Petrol was leaking out and I had to somehow get out. I asked God to help me. Suddenly, I felt the weight disappear and I was able to crawl out from under the bike. No one had lifted it.

Some months later, I was out in the paddock again. I'd been having a lot of treatment and was still feeling pretty bad. I looked across at the fence and saw two of my lambs there. Then suddenly, another lamb appeared alongside them. It wasn't one of mine – it was so amazingly white and perfect. And it still had its tail so it couldn't have been one of mine! I thought maybe someone had given me a sheep, but knew they hadn't. I stared at it for a long time and knew that it was telling me I was safe. Then suddenly it just disappeared. I never saw it again. But sometimes, I still look for it.

RAY SMITH

When I was nine, my grandmother Gertrude died. That's when I began to see ghosts. At that age, I didn't even know the word sanctuary but now the *knowledge* I have of such experiences in my life gives me a great sense of its mystery and sacredness. Here is a story I wrote about this first experience with ghosts. Although I wrote it as an adult, I adopted the voice of myself 'grown up' at 16, looking back on the innocence of childhood.

A Starling in the Northern Sky

I'd seen it at play-time – dark against a Salford sky, swirling around chimney smoke.

The curtains to our flat were closed – like the day our neighbour disappeared. That lightless afternoon when I worked out that disappearing meant death.

Mam was sat by the stove weeping. Her pinny was all wet down the front. There was a tray of burnt scones on top of the stove. She kept looking up at me, as if she was going to say something. I started to shake her. 'Mam! Mam! What's the matter? Mam!'

A dreadful heavy thing pressed down from the sky on my chest. I wanted to be grown up enough. So I said meaningfully, 'I saw a starling today, Mam. On its own.'

'Your Nana's dead. She died this morning. You'll have to go to Auntie Madeleine's for a while.' Nana dead. My nana. My nana dead.

That night, I looked up over the roof-tops at the stars, looking for that starling – to call it back. But it was too late. She had gone.

I wanted to go to the funeral but Mam said, 'No. There'll be enough of them when you're grown up.' 'I AM grown up!'

Nothing was the same after Nana died. Mam stopped dancing and wore black clothes. I heard her crying upstairs but I didn't know what to do. The days of helping her sew sequins on her skirts were over.

In spring, Mam took me to the cemetery to see the daffodils. We went every Saturday after that. We'd see who could spot Nana's headstone first. Our Lady of Lourdes. It stood out from the rest. We'd go past the church, and down the lanes of paupers' tombs. Lines and lines of oval-topped grey stones. All the same. Once we counted seventeen babies in one grave.

One afternoon, in a pauper's grave, we found Eliza, Mam's baby sister. Mam picked up a piece of slate from the path and scratched the name again and again, in a terrible rage, until the name stood out, whitened, from all the others. 'Eliza, 16 months, 1st June 1910.'

Not long after that, I started to see the ghosts. I'd see the paupers floating above the church, in the trees, watching me. When we went inside to light a candle, a ghost would make it flicker.

Whenever I stayed at Auntie's, I could hear breathing in the oak trees at night. I even saw the White Lady herself. Auntie had told me about her, but I'd never seen her myself till now. That's when I started to cross myself.

By Christmas, the ghosts were everywhere. They called down to me from the grime on the factory walls and winked up at me from the River Irwell. They even began to follow me to school, biting my heels as I ran.

I couldn't stop crossing myself. I even did it in assembly, just after the 'Our Father', and before the cod liver oil. We were a Proddidog school so I had to do it secretly. But one day Mr Small caught me out and dragged me to the front. He made me stand on a chair. 'Now look at this girl! Full of Popish nonsense! No one may speak to her today.' The hall hissed back: 'Catlicker!' 'Catlicker!' 'Catlicker!' Then he took out Betsy, his favourite cane, and started banging it on the desk.

Mr Small is very tall

He goes to church on Sundays.

He prays to God to give him strength

To thrash the kids on Mondays.

About a year later, I asked Auntie what really happened when Nana died. Auntie's a nurse and knows about these things. She knows when someone's going to die – she feels their fingers tapping on her shoulder. Sometimes she hears them calling from another ward. Sometimes they cry out from the asylum up the hill, and she runs through the night, with her red cape flying, to be with them at the end.

It's funny how you understand these things when you grow up. It all falls into place. I go into the fourth form next week and I've got my O-Levels this year. I'm doing quite well. I haven't crossed myself for over a year now.

We got my new uniform yesterday. I'm going to be in Mrs Woodhead's class. They say she's tough and you have to do piles of home work so I suppose I won't have much time for writing any more. So I thought I'd better get this down now, in case I forget. It seems important to remember how I lost my nana and learnt about dying.

I know she won't ever come back again, but whenever I see a single starling, I still look out for Nana. And sometimes, on a calm night, I hear her breathing in the trees.[62]

Knowing more than we know

For some years I ran a poetry class at a local resthome, for people severely disabled by a stroke, Parkinson's or Alzheimer's disease. This class showed me in so many ways that although we may lose our physical strength and mental prowess, our soul remains a sanctuary.

Often the poems I read aloud were ones my class had learned as children. Occasionally someone would ask me to find a poem they half remembered.

I was struck by how much they enjoyed rhythm and rhyme. They were listening to the *music* of poetry. We had special occasions, like the time I was asked to read the entire *Rubáiyát of Omar Khayyám*. So one winter's morning we lit candles, sipped mulled wine and imagined ourselves sitting on Persian carpets.

After the class had been running about three years, I suggested that we write a poetry book of our own. It seemed an outlandish idea, because most couldn't write, many had difficulty speaking, and several found concentration very hard, yet I was sure it was possible. Trish Howard, the diversional therapist who gave great support to volunteers at the resthome, was keen to be involved. Slowly, Trish and I helped people *find the words*.

A few people with advanced dementia wrote a poem as a group. I brought in objects which I thought they'd find interesting. We sat at a table, passing the objects around, feeling them, examining them. Trish and I scribbled down everything they said and later I put the phrases one after another. That is how these poems were made one day at Sevenoaks Lodge in Paraparaumu.

Looking at an Indian Box

I like the lining of this box.
Those two figures sitting, talking.
A man and a woman.
He is in earnest. This man will get answers.
There is a look of hope on both their faces.
They hope to have the very best.
They want to understand.
They are in a country inhabited by foreigners,
taken over from the original people.
No longer does it have the living
it used to. It's mostly lines
and somebody holding something.
I would keep a camera and film in this box.
I would keep cigarettes.
I would use the box to give some kind of answer.
This box will be valuable.

M.C., D.L., M.R., J.T.

One person was so taken with a carving I'd brought home from Easter Island that she wrote a poem alone. Remember, as you read, that her words came out painfully slowly and seemed unconnected when she said them.

Looking at a Statue from Easter Island

Studying it more, a little longer,
it's like a story-tale, giving out
whispers of days gone by.
I would like to have the days come back.
To tell the story of things
we are able to do.
It's a lovely piece of work.
One's almost breathless.
It moved me like this. I wanted to say it.

M.C.

One person had no written or spoken language yet seemed to love listening to the poems read in class. Would she be able to write a poem? We looked through pictures with her. We made cards of words associated with the pictures she liked and said them to her as we looked at the picture. Then we laid the cards, one by one, before her, slowly saying the word. If she pointed to a card we put it to one side, and at the end we laid those cards out on the table in front of her. She moved them around, as if making a pattern, and then she picked them up, one at a time, and gave them to me. I turned her first two words into the title, and added some punctuation. Apart from that, it is V's poem. Was the order random? I know she wasn't reading, but something was created that afternoon.

Age Struggle

The clock was my heart
Yesterday.
I sense, fear, wish.
Hours feel cold.
Try to arrive.
Listen.

V.E.

We made some copies of *Finding the Words* for the class and their friends and family. It was launched at an afternoon tea, with cream cakes and a red rose for every poet. Although no one could read their own poem aloud, every poem was read out. In fact, we were inundated by requests from staff to act as readers. The last poem in our book was the shortest poem, written by someone who had never said a word in class before, yet she summarised our entire project:

> *Perhaps I know more than I know myself.*
>
> G.R.

This class taught me so much about the power of the human spirit. It reassured me that the simplicity and delight of the child inside can stay with us forever. When someone glowed with pleasure, or clapped out a rhythm, I could see that child.

The child inside

Pat Cumming, one of the people in *A Gift of Stories*, told me that it was only when she got to know her inner child, 'Patrice', that she began to deal with the depression that stemmed from sexual abuse. 'It's helped me incredibly to get to know Patrice, and she's absolutely marvellous, she's so much fun. She's such a strong little girl, eh? And so brave. She likes Cowboys and Indians. She's got a big silver sheriff's badge that she wears.'[63]

I too have a sense of a child inside me. It is a part of the whole, a part still innocent, easily amazed, questioning and unreservedly loving. The child is close to the space within my heart. As long as I stay connected to her, I am connected to my spirit. Not only can I comfort the child, but the child can comfort me.

Rainy Day

Sometimes, I think of lives I might have known.
I still see streets I ran down in the rain,
chasing rainbows far away from home,
as if my time would never come again.
I walked into my life without a glance,
following whatever seemed most kind.
I didn't choose. I took the path of chance.
I don't remember making up my mind.
The girl inside, the one who raced down streets,
asks me if I found her pot of gold.
'Perhaps,' I say. In silence, our eyes meet.
She takes my hand. I know I'm getting old.
A rainy day. Today, I'm feeling sad.
Sometimes, I think of lives we might have had.[64]

Spirituality is space

A Quaker friend in England reflected on the way sanctuary, as a spiritual experience, permeates her entire life:

> Sanctuary is Home, Safety, Security, Protection … its immediate associations for me are extremely personal, and signify that goodness that comes from feeling at ease with myself and with others. My own home is a sanctuary to me, a cosy nest full of meaning and layered with possessions that are intrinsically appealing

to me and which, taken together, form a kind of narrative of my life. I often experience great self-doubt, anxiety and frustration, and my home harbours these feelings on my part too, but as a protective cocoon, enabling me to emerge renewed.

A loving family, friendships, religious belief and fellowship (for me found within the Society of Friends/Quakers) and other meaningful relations form a kind of social sanctuary too, physically in the form of other people or familiar places or shared customs, but also intangibly of the mind and heart … Sanctuary from what? Inner demons, outer dangers. Sanctuary in reading, in writing, in music and all the arts; delight in watching good documentaries or feature films; in making breakfast; in sharing my home; in the glories of the natural world – sunshine, blue sky, the miracle of Creation; in good health and whatever happiness we find. In seeing meaning in life; in the generations we span; in one another.

And so it seems, the more I ponder, that Sanctuary is a very fluid, encompassing concept and reality. It is a name for the shelter and succour we are fortunate to enjoy.

There's one word that sums up Sanctuary for me: Spiritual. My experience of sanctuary, whatsoever form it takes, has a direct line to my spirit.

MOLLY PORTER

When I reflect on my experiences of sanctuary, every one of them has some spiritual meaning for me. I can almost say that no experience of sanctuary exists for me unless there is a spiritual connection.

In the first section of the book, I told my own story about making space as a way to survive illness. At that time in my life I felt that spirituality was space.

Sometimes our ideas change and slip into different ones without our even seeing it happen. But the idea I had back then that spirituality is space itself has remained with me, intact and strong. Every aspect of my contemplation on sanctuary has pointed me in the same direction. Sanctuary is a sacred space, and simply by *being* there, I am safe.

time for time

It always seems mysterious that we can't see a truly new moon. Here is a new moon a couple of days old. Moon tables tell me that when I took this photograph it was just over an hour until the moon would set. Three hours earlier, it was 366,054 kilometres away from where I stood. Not so far, really. Raumati, 2009.

Clocking in

I was born into a home of time fighters. The clock on the mantelpiece was always set a quarter of an hour fast. Mum said it was so that we would have plenty of time. Dad used to joke, 'Take your time and hurry up.' Gran, Dad's mum, would come through the door mimicking the northern comedian Ken Platt, saying, 'I won't take m'coat off. I'm not stoppin'.'

I have been running ever since I was a child, and as an adult still struggle with 'hurry sickness' – a generalised, free-floating anxiety that converges on the feeling that 'I don't have enough time'.

I haven't worn a watch since I was in my thirties yet usually know the time precisely. After my dad died, I wore his old watch for a while. It had stopped going and couldn't be mended but when I put it on, it started ticking. I suppose it was Dad again, telling me to hurry up.

At home, Doug and I have one alarm clock and 11 digital clocks, which some manufacturer of stovetop, oven, microwave, computer, television, CD player, video, radio and cellphone thought we couldn't live without. I just went around to count them. There's no getting away from clocks and they continuously tell us that there are 24 hours in the day and 60 minutes in each of them.

There is only one clock I like – the grandfather clock in our lounge. It has a beautiful face, and even though it chimes on the hour and half hour, I find its tone of voice comforting. It's never pressing. We have a *relationship* with this clock. If we don't look after it, it will stop. So we give it permission to make us aware of the passing of time.

Talking about time

We can learn a lot about relationships from how we talk about someone, or some*thing*. Consider how we talk about time. We try to find it, take it and make it. We have time to spare, burn and while away. Sometimes we just have time on our hands. Other times, it drags. We might pass the time of day or mind time, keep it, mark it, beat it, or play for it until our time's up. Then again, we might just put it aside.

Sometimes we have the time of our lives despite our time of life. We work against time, and occupy it. We fill it or kill it. We buy, borrow, gain, seize and steal it. We waste it and fritter it away. We spend it, are short of it, run out of it and lose it. And what if we run out of prime time, peak time or quality time?

We have no time for someone we don't like. We know when it's high time to do something and we do it in the nick of time or wait for the fullness of time. Sometimes we are just time-worn and need to take time out or time off. Otherwise we just have to keep going – in the meantime.

Time is a line, circle, wheel, spiral. It is a bird that flies, a stream that flows, a river that runs, sands that run out, or an arrow flying towards a target. It is a soldier that marches on, a scythe that cuts us down, an old father, and a healer.

Allocating time

We treat time as if were a financial commodity. We've got just so much in the bank and we can spend it as we wish but it's going to run out at some point. For example, if I live to 75, I will have been allocated 657,000 hours.[65] That seems quite a lot.

Yet I'll probably spend 219,000 hours sleeping, 219,000 in education or working, 54,750 on chores, 82,125 on washing, eating and going to the toilet, 27,375 on getting around. I'll only have 54,750 hours of 'free time' in my entire life! When I think of it like that, it makes spending seven hours a week walking on the beach seem quite expensive. Or does it?

All our lives, we have an ambivalent relationship with time. It is as if we must use time well and never take it for granted, yet must not be its slave. Do *we* use time or does time use *us*? Maybe we treat our *measure* of time as if it were time itself?

A closer relationship with time

We have quite a personal relationship with time, which changes with our mood and circumstances, and with our age. We even have *feelings* about time, an emotional relationship, if you like. We can see it as our friend or as our enemy.

Journal, November 2006

There is one word bigger than love, and it is time. It does not pass us by or slide invisibly along the skin of life. It takes us in its arms in a passionate embrace and squeezes us to death.

Time is our friend and our enemy, the be all and end all of life.

Time is a single word that lights and blows us out, leaving a space where a trail of smoke might linger.

We notice time through *seeing* and *hearing* time but we don't talk of *smelling* time. Yet, in the garden, when I smell the green of growth, I feel closer to time. On the beach, the scent of salt air at high tide exhilarates me with the buoyancy of time. Do I taste time in a Lancashire hot-pot, cooked overnight for 12 hours? Sometimes, we talk about *feeling* time when we sense it slipping away, or racing ahead. When I take my own pulse, I am *touching* time, *touched* by time.

Different cultures have different relationships with time. Many Eastern cultures see time as circular, continually renewing itself. Western cultures view it as linear, so that time is always draining away.[66]

What if we were to get in touch with more primitive feelings? Would our relationship have a different meaning – perhaps a deeper, freer one? Would we begin to see time as energy, as a source of renewal in our life, rather than something foreshadowing our death?

When I focus on the progress of the sun, and feel changes in temperature, and notice the lengthening shadows, I am much more in touch with time. When I follow the movement of the constellations over the seasons, I feel at one with time.

I am a moon-watcher and follow the cyclic phases of the moon. It gives me my strongest *sense* of time. Over time, I can even feel I am *part* of time.

Journal, July 2011, Kopua

Waiting for the moon to rise last night, I couldn't see it at first, but knew it was there. Instead, I watched the constellations and Scorpius kept me company. I went inside for a moment and out it came! I saw it through the window. Your shy, beautiful moon.

The sanctuary of the moon

On the night of 19–20 March 2011 there was a 'moon event'. The moon was to be closer to the earth than it had been for 17 years. It was equinox, when day and night are in perfect balance, and it was a full moon, a time I feel a certain energy.

I went down to the beach before sunrise to watch it set into the sea. A friend who is also a moon watcher turned up at the same part of the beach and we watched the moon set together. Two people, sitting on a beach, watching a giant moon, talked of their relationship with the moon, as the sun rose behind them.

We discussed what the phases of the moon meant to us. My friend has learned over the years that her flows of energy are in line with the phases of the moon and had begun to use the Māori calendar, which is a lunar calendar, to structure her life.[67] I told her that during the past two years I had been following the Jewish calendar, also lunar.

The moon is far more personal to me than the sun. It doesn't surprise me that the moon is often spoken of in human terms. The new moon cannot be seen except 'in the arms of the old', as if the moon can cradle itself. I see the moon as a metaphor for life. It is cyclical. It waxes and wanes, continually renewing. It is sometimes illuminated, sometimes concealed. It can be mysterious, subtle, romantic. It can be clear, cold, distant. The moon goes through phases, a word that comes from Greek *phasis* meaning appearance. Just like life: what we see is not all that there is. I often dream about the moon.

> ***Journal, January 2011***
>
> *I had a wonderful dream last night. I was on a journey on a country road. There was someone in the distance trying to get my attention. They shouted out, 'Look at the moons!' I looked up and there, in a blue sky, high above the green hills, were four moons. Two of them were full moons and two of them were slivers of new moons.*

The sanctuary of the seasons

Just like following the cycles of the moon, when we are closely aware of the seasons, we can sense when to withdraw and conserve energy, and when to emerge and use it. Perhaps we have a strong connection with the season in which we were born. My month is November and I was born in an English autumn. I have always felt that I am a child of autumn and I belong to autumn.

Moving from the northern to the southern hemisphere was very disturbing on many levels. One of them was to do with seasons. Here in New Zealand, my birthday falls just after the spring bulbs have flowered, with summer around the corner. It doesn't make *sense* to me. I understand it, but it *feels* wrong. It always has.

As a child of the north, my blood was infused with rich autumn legends. Halloween, when the spirit world comes closer to the earthly world; Bonfire Night, 'a penny for the guy', fireworks and treacle ('treason') toffee, crowding around flames as the bonfire lights up the cobblestones; Harvest Festival, with the church full of fruit and vegetables. *My* time of year.

I love being in the autumn of my life, and know that is why I am writing this book now. I am harvesting my experiences of life. Autumn is golden, rich and deep, when things fall from the sky to earth in abundance: rain, leaves, apples, nuts. A time of plenty.

I have a strong primitive sense of preparing for hibernation. By early autumn, I am bottling our plums and peaches and making jam to store in the pantry. I get serious about soup and make sure the woodpile is high enough. I prune dead branches and gather kindling. Late autumn is relief, release. It moves from plenty to a time of drawing in. I want to hide in bushes, disappear in mounds of leaves, and breathe more slowly. I breathe a sigh of relief as the days get shorter and closer to the ease of night. Soon, it will be time to go inside.

Winter is withdrawal, when we can go into ourselves for introspection, intimacy, slowness, warmth and waiting. In winter, I want to stop doing things. Stay home. Stay warm. Sleep more. Winter is a cocoon, a womb, a place to retreat and live by the heartbeat. Things are slower and, just like the garden, I conserve my strength for the next round of growth. And just like in the garden, some things do not survive the cold. Some things do not wake up from the long sleep.

Spring is vigorous, turbulent, dynamic. It delights and disturbs me. The garden demands attention, care, admiration. It's time for light, for freshness, for getting ready for summer.

Journal, first day of spring, 2010

I am sifting through myself, looking closely into some of the corners, shining a torch where it is too dark to see, brushing away the spiders' webs and opening the windows. I pick up ornaments and polish them and put them in high places so I can see them all the time. It is important to have been to, and seen to, every corner of this house. I throw away the things I don't need any more, to make space for new. I repair what's broken, mend what's torn, throw out what's 'neither use nor ornament', as Gran used to say.

Summer is not my natural time at all and it has taken me a long time to know how to enjoy a summer. I used to watch the world having fun in summer in ways that I never felt part of. As I have grown older, I have discovered my own kind of summer. The best days are completely sensory: on the garden swing, reading, sipping wine, listening to the cicadas, or spent down at the beach, deep in the waves – the embodiment of joy.

The sanctuary of darkness

When does a new day begin? Is it at midnight, as the clock says, or is at it at dawn, when we see first light? Or does the day begin shortly after sunset, as in the Jewish and Islamic world? Over the last few years, I have been getting used to the idea that day begins with the onset of dark when I can see three stars in the sky. This opening of day is an enigmatic reminder that there is dark *before* there is light.

Dark is not just an absence of light. It is something in its own right. There are colours in darkness that do not need light. Jay Litvin writes about this kind of darkness:

> Imagine this darkness not as the absence of light, but as a thing unto itself. Stuff of a different consistency to light. For a different purpose, but a purpose all its own. This darkness surrounds you, awaits you, offers itself to you. It is what allows you to be; it is

> material from which you can create the world. The darkness of which I speak is the playground of the imagination, of creativity, of your deepest self … It is your friend, an ally that is willing to be whatever you wish or need it to be. Sometimes it becomes things you'd rather it not, but which you need it to be from a part of yourself deeper than the self that thinks it knows what it needs.[68]

Dark is the unknown. You cannot see what is there and cannot predict what you will find. Sometimes I am afraid of the dark, yet still drawn to the depths beyond consciousness. It's in my nature to dive beneath the surface, into that cold water, and try to swim. Sometimes, it is dangerously exhausting. Sometimes it is like being in an ocean of light.

At Kopua, the offices of Compline and Vigils mark the edges of darkness and enclose the sanctuary of night. I stand for a moment under the night sky and know my spirit is infinite. It is as if the night pulls me in until I belong to the universe.

The first time I went to Kopua I came across the following poem, which the Abbot, Brian Keogh, had included in a beautiful service sheet about Compline. Ever since reading this, I have understood that Compline, which completes day, is about entering the embrace of darkness. The German poet Rainer Maria Rilke's insight that darkness includes everything and everyone – in a way that light does not – is astonishingly powerful.

You, Darkness

You, darkness, of whom I am born –
I love you more than the flame
that limits the world
to the circle it illumines
and excludes all the rest.
But the dark embraces everything:
shapes and shadows, creatures and me, people,
nations – just as they are.
It lets me imagine
a great presence stirring beside me.
I believe in the night.

RAINER MARIA RILKE[69]

Rilke's poem evokes and assuages our primordial fears. He draws everything together in the embrace of dark: shapes, shadows and animals. The very things we most fear, at some primitive level, are brought close to us as we are all held together in the sanctuary of night.

Vigils, the 'night watch', begin at 4 am. It is still dark as I cross from the guesthouse to the church and there are so many visible stars in the countryside of Kopua. In winter the monks are often already in the choir stalls with their black pointed hoods up. It is like stepping into the Middle Ages.

Journal, All Souls' Day, 2011, Kopua

This night the ones who are not there, are here, when we remember them; the journey of their souls not yet begun. They wait, as we do, in a vigil for the dawn, the gate is not yet open, yet not shut. Like any threshold everything is lost and found, wanted and not wanted, and we can only watch them, from afar.

Rooks in fields are flying into owls, and rabbits are mistaking ducks for dawn. The stars are out but still we cannot see the oldest ghosts. Hermits stand back, eyeing us by and by.

An old monk rises and pulls on his tunic and tries not to curse the dawn. His turn to light the lamps and set the pews and he longs to dream a little more, pulling on his beard to remember the lad he was in Ireland.

Meanwhile all the souls are waiting for our prayers.

The chants begin, the psalms are open-handed.

God is listening.

We are here.

I love the *symmetry* of Vigils: three psalms, a reading and response; three psalms, a reading and response. It reflects the pattern of Christian night and day. The first reading is from the Old Testament, the second from the New Testament. It is the most orderly of all the services, the one with most constraint, the one I find most soothing. On some of my visits to Kopua, crossing from the church back to the guesthouse after Vigils, I see the Morning Star, I hear a morepork.

David Steindl-Rast and Sharon Lebell have produced a beautiful and lyrical modern exposition of the canonical hours, called *The Music of Silence*:

> The message of the house is to live daily with the *real* rhythms of the day. To live responsively, consciously, and intentionally directing our lives from within, not being swept along by the demands of the clock, by external agenda, by mere reactions to whatever happens. By living in the real rhythms, we ourselves become more real.[70]

The sanctuary of light

Before sunset on a Friday, I light the candles of *Shabbat*. This is the most sacred time of the week – when the connection with God is at its most direct. It is a time to let go of anxieties and cares: a time not to be distracted by work or earthly concerns. It is a time of enlightenment; a time to experience the grace of being: a sacred space. I turn off the phones and computer and spend the day quietly at home. *Shabbat* is a sanctuary of time that protects me from day-to-day concerns – *as long as I protect it.*

Friday night is the highlight of my week. I observe *Shabbat* as well as I may, given I am not Jewish. I love baking *challah* and laying the table, and making a good meal. We are often joined by friends. I sing 'Shalom Aleichem' (a song to welcome the angels of *Shabbat*) and Doug makes *kiddush* (the blessing over wine and bread) and, after the meal, our friend Christine says the grace. Then Doug reads to us, usually from the Torah.

Journal, April 2011

A perfect day in the midst of troubled times. An oasis – Shabbos.

It began with such a lovely evening last night – the candles, prayers, company, meal and readings.

No wind and one of those cold sunny autumn mornings. This morning I walked on the beach. A wide ocean, a few boats setting off towards Kapiti, and one or two walkers and dogs. So incredibly still, blue-grey, magic.

Then a day of silence – Doug was out all afternoon playing croquet. I just rested in the day and it was not marked by time at all. The day just stretched out and so did I – like being in the sea, on a slow wave, all day long. Deeply, deeply satisfying. As if I were taking deep breaths all day without knowing it.

Abraham Heschel, who was Professor of Ethics and Mysticism at the Jewish Theological Seminary of America from the 1940s–1970s, believed that the idea of a sabbath is one of the most spiritually powerful concepts in the world of thought. In his exquisite meditation on the meaning and experience of *Shabbat*, he unfolds the idea that 'Judaism is *a religion of time* aiming at the *sanctification of time*.'[71]

He explains that in Judaism there are few sacred places, but numerous sacred times. There is only one Temple, but many synagogues. The very idea of sanctuary in Jewish tradition is something *portable*, not fixed. It is something carried *within us*, throughout time. This means that time itself is sacred.

Rabbi Schlomo Carlebach, a charismatic teacher, composer and singer, called *Shabbat* the highest energy centre in the world. 'It's not a day when you're not doing anything. *Shabbat* is the day when your soul is at the most, most high.

What's the most precious possession of a human being? According to Rebbe Nachman, it's our thoughts, what we can imagine with our minds and hearts.'[72]

On a Saturday night, when I can see three stars in the sky, I light a candle during the Havdalah ceremony, which marks the end of *Shabbat* and the separation between the holy and the secular. It is a comforting ceremony, which connects me to all my senses. I hear the prayer, see the shadow of my fingers after lighting a candle, feel its heat, smell the spices and taste the wine, each time with a blessing. 'Paradoxically, this act of separation is what *connects* Shabbat with the rest of the week. When the boundaries between the holy and the ordinary are blurred, the holy is no longer holy and the ordinary is left with nothing to uplift it.'[73]

The sanctuary of New Year

Standing on the edge of a new year, I see a sanctuary of possibility. I have always seen New Year as a chance to review, renew, discover, and develop. Standing on the shoulders of the past, I see it as a new beginning, every year, year after year. New Year is full of mystery, meaning and miracle.

Journal, New Year's Day, 2003

Auntie used to say, 'It'll come in of its own accord'. And here's me thinking you had to bring it in. Usher it in. Welcome. Make a fuss. When I was little, I used to think Auntie stayed in the old year, because she never brought in the new one!

It's always been special for me. The main night of the year, far beyond baubles or the cribs of Christmas. The moment of choice. Now we are there, now we are here, with the chance to be different. Clean sheet. New paper. Fresh ink.

Outside the midnight wailers. Wild sounds of some other time and place. In churches the creaking bones of saints shake in time to plainchant. Wake up the day. Be bold. Behold the Day. Relate your selves. We bring our own traditions.

I take out the old and bring in the new:

Bread so you won't go hungry

Salt so you won't be poor

Coal so you'll be warm.

But it wasn't coal. There's none round here. Just driftwood off the beach at Raumati. A make-do kind of ritual. But the heart was there and a bit of my past and soul inside my parcel.

Dad used to go out just before midnight. Mum would get the port ready. Tiny glasses, a tipple for each. I think the same bottle lasted my whole childhood.

We'd hear the bells and there he was in the snow, knocking on the door. And such a thing it was – Dad with his parcel of hope for the New Year and our hugs and clinking of glasses! Something to remember for always. All time. Every new year. As long as I live. The gift of an indelible memory. One of the greatest gifts we have.

Port, the colour of jewels and blood. Rich and ruby. Special. Warming the cockles of any heart. But where did I put the cockles? And what did I think they were?

The years rushed by and on the edge I stood waiting for my port. My ship coming home. Docking. My landing. My aft to stern commitment to life. My need to do it every year. To say. There is a chance. Let us reflect. Break bread. Commit ourselves to more communion with life.

Outside the crowds run around on streets like slips of paper looking for words. Love. Sex. Fun and possibility. The sharp cut of the soul to say we're here, knocking on the door of the heart. Some light candles. Some close their eyes. Some get drunk and anaesthetise themselves from self-recognition.

What is it I want? To sit in a circle with those who matter and say we are here. We were. We are. We will be. To recognise our sacred self – the human heart. Some point of touch. Be touched. Any heart. Any home. Any harbour. Somewhere the cockles lie.

In recent years, I have come to recognise another New Year, *Rosh Hashana*, the Jewish New Year. Now, everything I have always intuitively known about the significance of a new year makes even more sense.

Journal, September 2011, Kopua

It is a few days before Rosh Hashana and the start of the Days of Awe. To be in awe of something – to fear it and also be full of wonder.

It's strange to be at Kopua at this time, but I was offered this space and walked through the open door. Brother Tony brought me a copy of The Hebrew Bible again. To be accepted as I am is such a gift of love.

The last day of this sanctuary of time is Yom Kippur – the Day of Atonement. During these Ten Days of Awe, I must perform teshuvah, *which is the act of repentance and literally means return – to turn back to one's true essence. To the person my soul wants me to be. To return to the source of life. To come home.*

To come home, I have to 're-turn'. I have to go back.

I am reflecting on the past year and thinking about the things I wish I'd done differently, people I hurt, things I might be able to put right. I couldn't do this if I never thought of the past. I plan to have the Rosh Hashana meal in one of the garden houses and need to find the best place to get down to the river for the tashlikh *ceremony, to empty my pockets of crumbs of bread into flowing water, symbolically casting away the sins of the past year.*[74]

Past present future

Why do we make such a sharp distinction between past, present and future? Maybe they are not as distinct as we think. Maybe the distinction comes from our perspective. What if we use the magical thinking of childhood – when we shut our eyes we are invisible. So if we close our eyes to time we are timeless. We are independent of time (and so, eternal) and unaffected by time (and so, ageless).

This is the kind of sanctuary I only know about afterwards, when I realise that time has passed and I have just spent time being – the being time. I might see a patch of garden, newly weeded, and suddenly become aware that I have been unaware of time and self. This sanctuary is transcendental – by that I mean it takes me away from and beyond myself into a state of being, essence, breathing, into dreams or daydreams. What happens to my mind in these states? Sometimes I wonder if such times can be actual experiences if I can't remember them. But of course they are, because the body can remember even when the conscious mind cannot.

I have friends who say they don't want to think about the past: there's no point, it's been and gone; it's too painful to revisit. I agree that sometimes the past is so painful that I don't want to revisit it. The trouble is that emotions buried alive never die, and when we search for meaning, we sometimes have to dig those emotions up again. We might be captured by them for a while. We might even need help with this.

Despite this, in my own experience I need to visit the past when I am looking for meaning in my life. Without looking back, I cannot say that this encounter was of value; that moment mattered; this was love; that was danger. My life is more meaningful when I live within the continuousness of time.

I also have friends who say they don't want to think about the future: scary, can't see the way ahead, one day at a time. I find thinking about the future far more challenging than the past, yet I can't imagine *not* thinking about it.

One night recently, a friend said over dinner, 'We think time only exists in the *present*.' This triggered a lot of contemplation for me in the days to follow. To act as if the future doesn't exist until it *becomes* present is to imagine it doesn't have a life of its own. As if time only exists in relation to *myself*, as if time had to enter *my* world to become real. It would also mean believing that I exist only in the present. But this present was once only known to me as the future; I just hadn't met myself yet.

I can't imagine *not* thinking about the past and the future because they are here in the present. If I don't remember the past and don't imagine a future, why bother living at all? The past has made me as I am and I can't leave it behind, it travels within me and I live on within it. Yet I change.

Even thinking of time as three separate entities – past, present and future – denies the ultimate sanctuary of time. I am just like time itself. In any one moment, time is past, present and future. So am I.

The sanctuary of timelessness

When people talk about timeless moments in their lives they often say that they were 'in the present moment'. Ken McLeod sets a challenge in his book about the need to pay attention to being alive:

> Stop reading for a moment, and imagine that you are going to die in one minute. The last things you are going to experience are reading these pages, sitting in this room, thinking and feeling what you are thinking and feeling right now. This is the end of your life … You have no time to write a note or make a phone call. All you can do is experience what is, right now. This is a very simple exercise, but it is quite profound. It brings you into presence very quickly. You stop fighting, you stop needing, you stop being concerned with physical comfort, you stop wanting, you stop achieving, and you stop maintaining. Enlightenment, attainment, realisation all become meaningless. You are just present.[75]

My nephew Nick is a musician – like his father, brother, mother and stepmother. In response to my question about sanctuary he sent a beautiful reply that expresses how fragile and evanescent our perception of timelessness can be:

To me, sanctuary is something I am yet to fully achieve. It is a time and a place and a sensory experience all woven together to produce a feeling of comfort, contentment and some other intangible. I say I am yet to achieve it, but this is not strictly true; I do experience fleeting moments that can last just a few seconds – when the light from the sun shines in the window in a particular way, catching the smoke from my cigarette and making transient smoke sculptures that have never existed before and never will again, and a particular song is playing, and I smell a particular perfume and have a particular feeling – something that in Western terms would be described as 'nostalgia', but really is nothing of the sort. I don't believe we have a word for it, but sanctuary is close enough. It is also appropriate, since I would most likely not notice the convergence of all these things, were I not somewhere I feel safe and almost sacred (though the sacred nature itself is only invoked by the convergence of sensory experience, memory and, for instance, a sudden awareness of a potential future of which I was unaware before this moment).

NICK ANTHONY

Nick's sister, my niece Amy, also wrote about sanctuary as a concept connected with time – and possibly with eternity.

Sanctuary does not necessarily have to be a place. It can be an inanimate object, another living organism, a thought, a memory, anything that gives you a sense of inner tranquillity. It might just be a secluded place where you feel comfortable, such as your bedroom, or a place of worship or astonishing natural beauty in which you feel close to God or connected to nature. You might feel that God Himself is the best sanctuary of all. However, I believe the most important element to sanctuary is safety. It is something that brings you a sense of acceptance, both of yourself and your circumstances. At the same time you feel as though you are being accepted, that you are not alone but are being understood and listened to.

Sanctuary can be a friendly smile or a comforting shoulder to cry on, or maybe a much-loved book or poem. Music, too, is something many people (including myself) find solace in, and thus could be described as a sort of sanctuary.

I think another aspect of sanctuary is that it endures. You can turn to it any time and it will always have the same innate qualities as it did when it first gave you peace of mind, even if its surface has changed over time.

On the whole, sanctuary is something that allows your heart and mind to breathe. You don't have to struggle with yourself or put on any silly pretensions there, because you feel no need to. You can just be, without dwelling on past pains or agonising over questions of what the future holds. In fact, you are so grounded in your present that the concept of time ceases to have any meaning. You almost feel you could stay in that place, or with that person or object, for an eternity.

AMY HALSTEAD

Only when I let go of the concept of time as something outside of myself is time a sanctuary. Then I become *indistinguishable* from time – so much in synchrony that time ceases to be an 'it'. I have an image somewhere in my head but it's not very well formed. In it, I am travelling on time itself, and so I am part of time. Then, there *is* no present moment any more than there are past or future moments. It is like making time itself timeless. I cannot *make* this happen. All I can do is be prepared, stand on some threshold, and if I cross over, then so be it.

protecting sanctuary

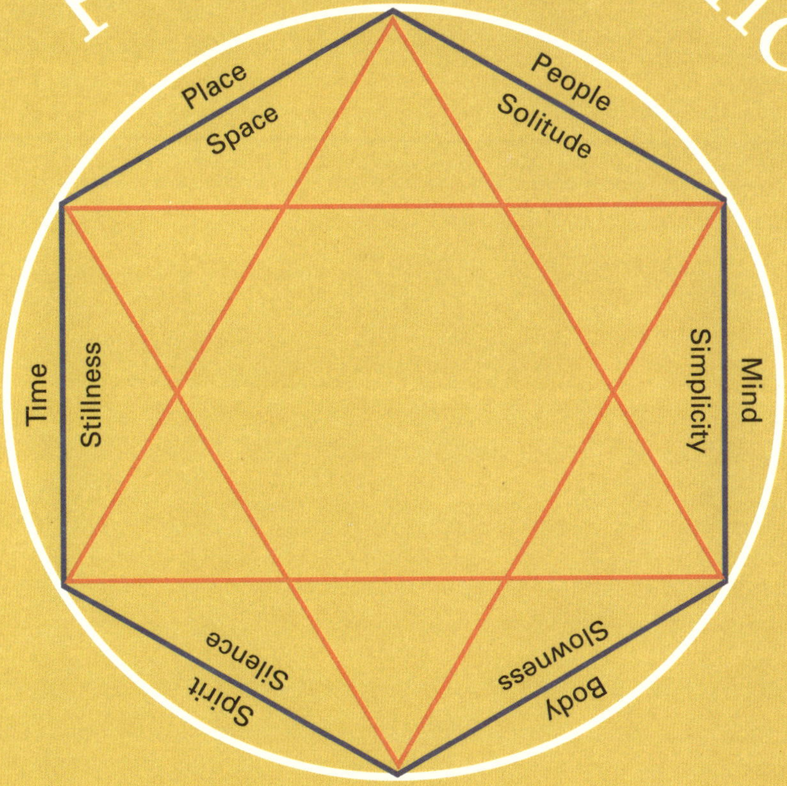

When a cloud passes in front of the moon, people say the moon is hiding behind a cloud. It's like sanctuary: we think it is hiding from us, when really we are obscuring it. Raumati, 2011.

space for space

Sanctuary is a self-made place. You can make it wherever you are. When I was about seven, on a June morning, in a little square patch of garden at the back of a three-storey house – those dark blue-black tiles around the edge of the flowerbeds – I was standing on tiptoe looking into a rose – pinky, yellow, cream, almost melting into a lighter cream. As you look inside there's a glistening dewdrop, somewhere on a petal. I was sinking into this rose, looking deeper and deeper, thinking that is where God must be.

DORIS SMEATON

Protecting that which protects

When I open the door to the space within, it's like going home, with a fire blazing in the hearth and someone welcoming me with open arms. There's nowhere in the world like it, because it doesn't depend on circumstance, schedule, mood or human frailty. It happens every time I go through the door.

I want to be able to enter this sacred space at any time, anywhere in the world, in the face of crowds, noise, rush, complexity and busy-ness, because it protects me. It has taken me a long time to realise that I have to protect that which protects me. The sacred space within is the most precious thing in my life so it is important to cherish it.

Just as I need time to become time, I need space to become space. I know, from experience, that this happens most easily when I make space to be alone, silent, slow, simple and still, in my external world. Then I am more likely to enter the space within. The more I practise entering, the stronger my connection will be to my inner world. A friend who is a hymn writer sees this inner world as a space where the soul can fly.

A spirit space. Somewhere – not so much a place as a spirit space – not to be touched. A safe space to be, think, play around in, re-collect, re-connect, grow perhaps. An essential escape place for freedom of soul to fly. As in the space of a cathedral or church, in times when outlaws begged at the door for entry, there's still a feeling of desperation associated with the word – that I need a place to run to. And that here I can juggle dangerous or mad ideas with impunity. Creating a little world within but away from the world, to deal with my world and people and thought. Or to forget the lot! Sometimes small and intimately contained, like a lighted cell. Sometimes opening out to a wide sky and air. Flying, floating. Simply to be, to be in stillness. Not even music. 'God and the imagination are one,' (Wallace Stevens). Just a thought that passed by.

SHIRLEY ERENA MURRAY

Space in society

Space as a term can bring up associations of the open, ample and generous, but it can also be seen as empty, gaping and barren. Perhaps we have a deep and primitive fear of being engulfed by space itself, consumed by infinite emptiness. Often, I still ignore my soul or take it for granted. I become seduced by being busy and then overwhelmed by the busy-ness of being. Sometimes I find myself resisting those practices that strengthen my sanctuary within.

Just like the term 'space', solitude, simplicity, slowness, stillness and silence are all double-edged concepts that can attract or repel, depending on the attributes we give them.

Journal, August 2008

All around there are noises and vibrations, pressings and demands while time is clocking in. There are myriad gates and fences and buses and trains and escalators to places I don't want to be. I see people running faster and faster and still not getting to where they want to be. Lines don't stay in place unless they are etched in the earth. Even then, there are earthquakes.

Why do we not seek space any more? Why do we fill our days with trivia, clutter our houses with possessions, and fill our lives with contacts rather than connections? Is it that space is too frightening? Is it dark? Does it mean absence? Will we lose our way? What if we need to lose our way to find ourselves?

Although we may acknowledge the importance of making space in our lives, we often continue to fill our lives with too many things, *leaving no space*. Even when I am overwhelmed and drowning in detail, I sometimes struggle on, trying to go faster and faster, filling every moment, as if I can outrun time. Sometimes I continue struggling until brought to an abrupt halt by an apparently external event – accident or illness.

I live in a society where it is becoming the norm to be continuously 'on show'. It is as if we believe that if we fill every crevice with activity, we will avoid emptiness in our lives. If we let others know about our busyness, they will see how full and vibrant our lives are.

Journal, October 2011

I woke thinking about the 'interiority' of life before the new age of show and tell. It's as if all the doors have been thrown open, the curtains drawn back, and the tops cut off our heads revealing our brains. It is as if there should be no solely interior life any more. Every trivial detail must be seen and shared. Facebook, Twitter, iPhones, cameras. Photographed and displayed. Reported and commented upon. Breathlessly. So fast there is no chance to be in the moment itself. We are being encouraged to live solely in order to record it for the entertainment of others.

We have to have countless friends, especially new ones, with torch-lights in their hands. The world has become a kaleidoscope of everyone's experiences, narrow, wide, deep and shallow. Mostly shallow. We show and speak and move our lips and smile. Much smiling happens now. It's a shiny, polished life. A hall of mirrors and we don't seem to care if they are distorted. The thing is to shine. Above all, we must shine.

We are supposed to cut out our hearts and paste them on our faces. The inner self, the person inside, the one who is scared and real daren't come out any more. Scared of light rather than dark. If we are not careful we will not recognise ourselves any more. What will happen if, in the rush to present ourselves, the distance between our private and public self becomes so great that we lose the ability to be authentic in any relationship?

Fears of making space

Why, so often, do I not make space when I need to, before I am forced to? Am I afraid of some social judgement that I am not productive enough? It is as if, in this society, we are always being urged to be somewhere else and someone else. And to *have* something else! Am I trying to seem important, needed or essential? Am I being driven by some early script about how to live my life? Do I think I will never be good enough for long enough to be loved? Am I avoiding facing something in my inner world? Could that something be emptiness? Maybe I am scared that my life is full of empty echoes.

Some of our most primitive fears are of emptiness, nothingness, a dark, void, limitless infinity of space. According to Charles Seife, in *Zero: The biography of a dangerous idea*, when the concept of zero was brought from the East to the West, it was so abhorrent that it was rejected and the Greeks would not use it in their writings, even though they could see its use. 'The reason: zero was dangerous … It is hard to imagine being afraid of a number: yet zero was inexorably linked with the void – with nothing. There was a primal fear of void and chaos. There was also a fear of zero.'[76]

Journal, January 2011

What if one is zero? What if zero is one? This is no riddle. I mean, what if being alone annihilates us? Where does emptying myself lead? What will it mean if I look in a mirror and no one looks back? Even worse, what if emptying myself of everything leads solely to myself?

It took seven centuries for the Aristotelian philosophy of the West to accept the existence of nothing. The confounding irony is that *to overcome emptiness, we need to become nothing.*

Becoming nothing

How can I give my soul what it needs to survive and flourish? By getting away from myself. The self shouts for attention whereas the soul whispers. The self gets in the way, juggling thoughts and emotions and actions all the time. I need to get rid of that inner observer: self-consciousness.

Journal, November, 2008

To be within time is to become time.
Nowhere, now here. Nothing, no thing.

It is only when I take time to become time that I am free of self.

It is only when I make space to become space that I am free of self.

They are one and the same experience.

What do I mean? I mean becoming nothing.

The idea of becoming nothing occurs in every spiritual tradition. I find it the most profound, powerful and elusive of all spiritual concepts. It has many names and comes in different guises: detachment from worldly things, detachment from self, relinquishing the ego, self-nullification, selflessness, humility. Jewish mystical writings refer to *ayin* or nothingness, Sufis refer to *al-baqa' ba'd al-fana'*, which means subsistence after annihilation. Meister Eckhart, a fourteenth-century German theologian and philosopher, expressed it like this:

> If you could naught yourself for an instant, indeed I say less than an instant, you would possess all that this is in itself. But as long as you mind anything at all, you know no more of God than my mouth knows of colour or my eye of taste.[77]

In *The River of Light*, Rabbi Lawrence Kushner explains: 'You cannot become someone other than you are until you are willing, just for a moment, to allow yourself to become one whom you are not. That is, until you are willing to enter Nothing. It is possibly the most effortless (and the most important) thing any of us can do.'[78]

To find inner space, we must free ourselves of all attachments. Only then can we make space for God. The self must detach itself from everything and then itself be emptied out. I can talk of this solely as a concept. It is not possible to talk about it as an experience, for how can the self know what it is like for the self to be eliminated?

Rabbi Aryeh Kaplan points to the infinite levels within this paradox in his books on Jewish meditation. One quotation within the books gave me a deeper insight into the paradox, in a way that I find very moving. The Maggid of Meseritch, a disciple of the Baal Shem Tov who founded the Chassidic movement, advised:

> Think of yourself as nothing, and totally forget yourself when you pray. Only have in mind that you are praying for the Divine Presence.
>
> You can then enter the Universe of Thought, a state that is beyond time. Everything in this realm is the same – life and death, land and sea …
>
> But in order to enter the Universe of Thought where all is the same, you must relinquish your ego, and forget all your troubles.
>
> You cannot reach this level if you attach yourself to physical, worldly things …
>
> Furthermore, if you consider yourself as 'something' and ask for your own needs, then God cannot clothe Himself in you. God is infinite and no vessel can hold him at all, except when a person makes himself like Nothing.[79]

Kabbalah, the name given to Jewish mysticism,[80] has at its very centre the concept of space. There is a fundamental belief that at the point of creation, God had to make space for the world. The mediaeval Jewish mystic Rabbi Isaac Luria (The Ari), one of the most holy and influential Jewish leaders, said God had to contract and conceal his energy so that there was space for the universe to be created. This contraction of energy is called *tzimtzum*:

> In the beginning, a simple divine light filled the entirety of existence … When there arose in His simple will the desire to create the worlds, He contracted His light, withdrawing it to the sides and leaving a void and an empty space in its centre, to allow for the existence of the worlds. (However, this was not an absolute void, for there remained a residue of the divine light within the void.) He then drew a single line of His infinite light into the void to illuminate the worlds.[81]

A contemplation on nothingness

Nothingness is not emptiness. Emptiness is about relationship with *self*. Nothingness is about relationship with *other*.

I imagine a globe.

Is the space inside emptiness, or nothingness? Emptiness.

Is the space outside emptiness or nothingness? Nothingness.

The globe is the only thing. Everything else is nothing, no thing. All things.

I imagine an egg in its shell, a baby in the

amniotic sac, a seed in a pod. Then the boundary dissolves and everything is space.

Space is the womb of creativity. If I contract myself into a point of timeless dark, the point opens out into infinite light.

Time, made by space, cannot be measured by time.

There are moments in my life, perhaps, when this has happened, but I can only find words to talk of the *readiness* to become space.

Maybe space is love? Maybe that is why detachment from self is the essence of love.

Something can only be created when there is space. Someone can only be born when there is space. We can only be renewed when there is space.

A children's story about nothing

In *The Biggest Number in the Universe*, Mr Abacus, a mathematician, helped a little girl called Nesta to count by demonstrating the importance of the number one.[82] Through this, Nesta came to see that she was unique. In its sequel, *Nesta and the Missing Zero*, Mr Abacus is very agitated, looking for something he has lost.[83] When Nesta asks him what he has lost, he says 'NOTHING!'

'But you said you'd lost SOMETHING!' she grizzles. 'I mean I've lost *zero*!' he replied with a sigh.

'Is zero important?' asked Nesta.
Mr Abacus plucked at his beard.
'It's a zip, a zilch, a zero,
a nothing and a naught,
an itsy bitsy circle
that can't be found or caught.
Add zero and you stay the same.
Take zero, you're still you.
It can't divide, but multiply
and you'll disappear from view!'
'Zero's must be a very odd number,' mused
Nesta.
'It's not odd! It's even!' barked Mr Abacus.
'But enough of this nonsense! We have to
find it!'

And so they go off in search of this nothing that is something. They search and search. They find somethings, anythings and even everythings but they never find nothing. Finally, Nesta becomes so frustrated that she says nothing doesn't exist.

Everything turns into chaos as zeros disappear from the face of the earth. Mr Abacus and all the numbers in the world call out for zero to return. The chaos becomes worse and worse until Nesta finally sees the power of nothing. She is desperate for it to come back and shouts out into the turmoil, 'I believe in you, Zero! Yes, I believe in nothing!'

It takes the voice of a child to restore meaning to the universe.

I like photographing silhouettes and shadows then hand washing the prints with watercolour; especially I love that moment when colours run into each other like old friends. Raumati, 2005.

company of solitude

> Inside myself is a place where I live all alone, and that's where I renew my springs that never dry up.
>
> PEARL BUCK[84]

> What a commentary on civilization, when being alone is being suspect; when one has to apologize for it, make excuses, hide the fact that one practices it – like a secret vice.
>
> ANNE MORROW LINDBERGH[85]

> Language … has created the word 'loneliness' to express the pain of being alone. And it has created the word 'solitude' to express the glory of being alone.
>
> PAUL TILLICH[86]

Solitude in society

Solitude is associated with peace, quiet, privacy and personal strength, but also with being cut off, friendless and forlorn. Solitude is often confused with loneliness. It is also confused with enforced isolation. In prisons, being put 'in solitary' is a punishment of confinement and segregation. In psychiatric hospitals the same punishment is called 'seclusion'.

From early on, children are judged on their ability to socialise with other children. Adults are measured on their ability to have many social connections. People who have very few friends are judged to be strange or withdrawn, or, as they get older, are seen as sad or having failed in life in some way. Society often represents people who live alone as isolated, lonely and even pitiable. It's as if our society thinks that being alone is wrong.

Social expectations in my own culture call for extensive interaction with others: it is essential to be part of a family and have lots of friends; you definitely need a partner and children; you should know your neighbours, stay in touch with your cousins, get involved with your community.

Modern technology encourages us in the illusion that we are never alone. It tricks people into thinking that they can continuously 'be in touch' with others, even if that means the touch of a button, rather than a heart. So much of what passes for communication nowadays isn't even contact, and certainly isn't connection.

Solitude, with its connotations of individuality, threatens conformity. There is something a bit secretive about solitude, something unknown, not shared. The group is society's strategic means of survival and so, in a sense, solitude threatens the fabric of society. Maybe there is a fear, at some fundamental level, that solitude is a rejection of society. I would like to illustrate this by looking at a curious literary tale.

One of the most famous accounts of solitude is Henry David Thoreau's experiment of living alone for two years in Walden Woods. He described his experience in *Walden*, first published in 1854: 'I went to the woods because I wished to live deliberately, to front only the essential facts of life, and see if I could not learn what it had to teach, and not, when I came to die, discover that I had not lived.'[87]

Thirty years later, Robert Louis Stevenson embarked on a character assassination of Thoreau. He opened a review in *Cornhill Magazine* in 1880 with a particular nastiness: 'Thoreau's thin, penetrating, big-nosed face, even in a bad woodcut, conveys some hint of the limitations of his mind and character.'[88] According to Stevenson, Thoreau was a self-righteous prig, avoiding real work. 'He did not wish virtue to go out of him among his fellow-men, but slunk into a corner to hoard it for himself.' It is as if Stevenson were personally offended or threatened by Thoreau's search for solitude.

Curiously, *Some Fruits of Solitude* by William Penn, an early Quaker and founder of Pennsylvania, was greatly treasured by Stevenson, who liked to carry around this compact little book of aphorisms, a summation of Penn's personal wisdom. 'There is not a man living – no, nor recently dead – that could put, with so lovely a spirit, so much honest, kind wisdom into words.'[89] I think he approved of Penn's book because it contained the *fruits* of solitude and was not about solitude itself. He saw Penn as generous but Thoreau as mean.

Was Thoreau a selfish man? Is it only acceptable for monks to be alone as long as they are busy praying for the world? Is it only admirable for explorers to go alone as long as they come back to tell us what they discovered? In any case, that is exactly what Thoreau did. He wrote of the *experience, the process,* of solitude and it took him eight years to complete his account. The day Thoreau walked into Walden Wood was a significant one for generations to come.

Fears of solitude

When I was about 12, I came across a book that suggested that our universe is a globe inside a much greater universe, which itself is a globe inside a much greater universe, which is a globe … I smell the polished oak of the library table as I read with a growing dread of infinite isolation seeping through me.

Shortly afterwards, I came across Jean Paul Sartre, and then fell over *The Outsider* by Albert Camus. That was nearly the finish of me. Then being 'an outsider' took on a romantic ambience for a while, and ran parallel to becoming an adolescent. Heathcliff, Jane Eyre and the Lady of Shalott somehow made it easier to deal with the struggles of growing up. Around this time my English teacher recognised my need for solitude and gave me a key to the book room – somewhere I could go 'to collect myself', as she called it.

My dad was a shy man and sometimes found company difficult. Mum, on the other hand, loved company and was extremely hospitable. She used to caution me, 'No man is an island.' Years later, I came across John Donne's Meditation XVII and the complete quotation:

> No man is an island, entire of itself; every man is a piece of the continent, a part of the main; if a clod be washed away by the sea, Europe is the less, as well as if a promontory were, as well as if a manor of thy friend's or of thine own were; any man's death diminishes me, because I am involved in mankind, and therefore never send to know for whom the bell tolls; it tolls for thee.[90]

Although it's hard to disagree with my favourite poet, I would use the island metaphor differently. Each of us is a separate island and the sea, not the land, connects us. What matters is that we are set in a spiritual sea and connected by that sea. Only when we forget that the sea exists do we become isolated.

The idea of existential loneliness repels yet also attracts me. That gives me a clue about why I am so interested in solitude. Its combination of danger and attraction is part of its inherent power.

Loneliness stems from unfulfilled longing for connection. I am rarely lonely for 'company', but sometimes I long to see a specific person. I may long to be with Doug, for instance, or to sit down for a deep conversation with a faraway friend. I may long for the physical presence of someone who has died. Most often, however, the connection that I long for is connection with my soul. I think back to the times I have locked myself out of my own sanctuary and couldn't get back in again. That is what existential loneliness is to me.

To be alone but not lonely is one of life's great challenges. The irony is that solitude is the cure for loneliness. As the theologian Paul Tillich said, 'Loneliness can be conquered only by those who can bear solitude.'[91] For as long as I can remember, I have used periods of solitude as a way of overcoming existential loneliness.

In solitude, thoughts and feelings that we were not aware of might come to the surface. It is mostly when we are physically alone that we face our demons. We might have the company of parts of our self we do not want around at all. There are times, alone and silent, my mind is still nattering alongside, nagging about things not done, people not seen. Sometimes memories crowd in, bringing rubbish I meant to leave in the past.

I suppose that many of us, if not all, have voices within that we'd rather not hear. They are the whisperers, cruel voices of our past that became buried inside us. The doubter, the frightened child, the shamed self. If I were to take notice of the voices for too long, I might not go on writing this book. I might let them convince me it's worthless, that I am not real, and my entire life is a façade. Yet the more I try to banish those voices, the stronger they become. The only way to deal with these voices is to notice them and recognise them for what they are, not fight them or run away from them, but let them wash over me like a passing rainstorm.

> ***Journal, July 2011, Kopua***
>
> *Love, why do I fear you? Even the pen is pulling back from the brink. Even this pen that I love, which makes words possible, is telling me to write on a dark page, in the dark so I can't see. I long for love, to love and be loved, but still hold back.*
>
> *The ink dries up.*
>
> *I fear love for what it can do in the name of love. Love hurts. It takes away. It occupies. I am ashamed to be so bleak. I want to speak of warmth and utter peace, to give, without holding back, receive and be received, in utter safety. I stumble to utter these words; my throat is dry. I cannot speak.*
>
> *My hand is moving as though it were not mine. I see the script before me and the page is full of tears.*

When I feel as I felt that day, the tears, the gooseflesh save me. The body tells the truth. There may be chasms that I think I can never cross, and yet I do. What I have to do, and can do best in solitude, is to draw those parts of myself that I most fear closer to the warmth of my fire. I need to bring them into the sanctuary within myself, so that they too are not afraid.

When I was younger, I sought solitude mainly as a way of dealing with depression – it was easier to be alone than to wear a cheerful mask. But gradually, through many experiences of being alone, there has been a transition; the nature of solitude has begun to change into a sense of intimate companionship.

The Companion

> ***Journal, March 2008***
>
> *Who emerges when I am alone? The Companion – someone I don't talk with as much as I need. Some inner self who holds the key to intuition.*
>
> *The one who was there at my birth. The one who will be there at my death. The only companion I will have all my life. This is the one who will never leave me, no matter what, not even at the end of this physical life. What an extraordinary relationship that is. One that must be treasured and protected.*

Sometimes, when I have been alone within myself for days at a time, it is as if The Companion writes:

Journal, October 2011, Kopua

I am here, waiting for you, and I won't ever leave you. We are one, you and I, we are one. We belong together. I made you and I love you. My child, my parent, my wife, my great love. I am your companion, your healer. I will make you whole.

Learning from others

In *Journal of a Solitude* American poet, novelist and memoirist May Sarton explains in exquisite detail the company of solitude. She disentangles the threads that can twist the need for solitude and the need for company into knots. It is the most revealing memoir I have read about solitude:

> I am here alone for the first time in weeks, to take up my 'real' life again at last. That is what is strange – that friends, even passionate love, are not my real life unless there is time alone in which to explore and discover what is happening or has happened. Without the interruptions, nourishing and maddening, this life would become arid. Yet I taste it fully only when I am alone here and the house and I resume old conversations.[92]

Some people like solitude more than others. Thinking of people I know who enjoy being alone, I would hazard they have some of these characteristics: they are writers, dreamers; people who want to look inwards and be undisturbed; people who need to be unseen, not demanded of; people who need to hide themselves; people who need to find themselves; people who *have* found themselves and enjoy the company of the self they have found.

Likewise, thinking of friends and acquaintances who prefer the company of others, I would hazard that they have at least one of these characteristics: they are planners, doers; they like to look outwards and ahead; they are comfortable in the presence of many people; and they like to feel involved, needed, active in the real world; they enjoy interaction.

According to Carl Jung's theory of personalities, some people get their energy from being alone, while for others it comes from being with people. The first group are called introverts, and the second extroverts. Maybe what matters is finding the balance between solitude and the company of others, and who is to say where the tipping point lies – except each individual?

In his book *Solitude: A return to the self*, British psychiatrist Anthony Storr challenges the 'modern insistence that true happiness can only be found in intimate attachments'. He gives numerous examples of people throughout history who found great happiness in solitude. 'Love and friendship are, of course, an important part of what makes life worthwhile. But they are not the only source of happiness.' 'Intimate attachments are *a* hub around which a person's life revolves, not necessarily *the* hub.'[93]

Storr illustrates, by describing the lives of artists, scientists, composers and authors, that solitude is an inherent part of many forms of creativity. He describes 'a capacity' that comes from inner security, and which brings many benefits such as the integration of ideas, abstraction, coherence and, perhaps most important, freedom of imagination. One of the striking features of Storr's analysis is that he is describing a self-fulfilling phenomenon: the more solitude we experience, the better being alone becomes.

At the end of *The Space within the Heart*, the book that was pivotal in recovering from my experience of psychiatric treatment, Aubrey Menen summarises the overall process of his search for the space within. He begins with the importance of finding and protecting the right *kind* of solitude. I return to this description from time to time and his homely, practical advice always makes me smile:

> Loneliness need not be harsh; there is no need to be an anchorite. In fact one must be very careful not to choose a hostile environment … The surroundings can be agreeable but not so much as to intrude … The next thing is to reduce the routine of living to its simplest terms, or better still, to have no routine at all … Vanities of dress and appearance must be abandoned, along with letters, telephone calls, newspaper and the like. Nor should too many people know what you are doing. Some must. Tell them not to seek you out. But others will, if you are not too far away. They will come thinking that your seclusion will have made you as sweet and saintly as a cloistered nun. Swear at them: it is the only thing to do; and the more vulgar your language, the more enduring will be its effect. When you have found the space within the heart, it is another matter. Then, nobody can take it away from you.[94]

The first time I went to Southern Star Abbey I had no idea what to do on a retreat. I quickly got the message to stop doing and just be. In the corridor of the old guesthouse at Kopua there was a magic bookshelf. Each time I went to Kopua, the book I most needed to read seemed to fall off the shelf into my hands. This is how I first met Thomas Merton, who became another imaginary friend, holding his hand out over time. And this friend certainly knew about solitude: 'It seems to me that solitude rips off all the masks and all the disguises. It tolerates no lies.'[95] John Barbour describes Merton's life-long struggle with two crucial issues about solitude:

He tried to understand how solitude can be combined with openness to other people and compassion for their suffering. And he wrestled with the question of right motivation, that is, how to discern when the desire for solitude springs from egotistical impulses and when it represents an authentic response to God's call.[96]

In her late eighties, Sister Jeremy Hall described her experiences as a Benedictine nun, having lived as a hermit for 20 years. She also addressed the idea of solitude being not just for oneself, but for the sake of the world: 'It is not about expanding the ego, but about losing it in the deeper self, the true self, and thus, again, nurturing the capacity for communion with others.'[97]

In *The Monastery*, a BBC television series, five men lived 'a monastic life' at a Benedictine monastery in Worth, England, for 40 days and nights, while cameras tracked their progress. I haven't viewed the series and can't quite imagine an *observed* solitude but the subsequent book by Abbot Christopher Jamison is warm and wise: 'To know yourself and to grow requires the insights that only solitude can provide. Even the most intimate friendship is no substitute for the work that we must all do on our own, the work of silent reflection and prayer.'[98]

Although solitude is not approved of as an end in itself in any religious tradition, examples abound of solitude as a way to spiritual growth. Consider the models we have: Moses went alone to Mount Sinai for 40 days and nights; Buddha sat in solitude and meditated for 49 days and nights; Jesus was alone in the wilderness for 40 days and nights, and Muhammad spent 40 days and nights alone in a cave on Mount Hira.[99]

Although Jewish tradition emphasises the importance of community,[100] the most influential Jewish mystics 'recommended practices of spiritual solitude, inner silence, and simplicity'.[101] Rabbi Isaac Luria meditated alone for six years, and the Rabbi Baal Shem Tov lived in solitary contemplation for many years, only rejoining his wife and family for *Shabbat*.[102]

Solitude goes hand in hand with being a mystic. It is almost a prerequisite. Many notable Christian mystics spent time as hermits: for example, the fourth-century Anthony of Egypt; the sixth-century St Benedict of Nursia and the fifteenth-century Julian of Norwich. Laozi, the sixth-century BCE mystic philosopher of ancient China and founder of Taoism, spent his final days as a hermit. Sufi mystics frequently write about the deep value of solitude:

> Which is worth more, a crowd of thousands,
> or your own genuine solitude?
> Freedom, or power over an entire nation?
> A little while alone in your room
> will prove more valuable than anything else
> that could ever be given you.
>
> JALĀL AD-DĪN MUHAMMAD RŪMĪ[103]

Joys of solitude

One day when I was about seven, I saw an advert in the local paper for garden sheds. Carefully, I cut around the dotted lines, filled in the form, found a stamp and posted it. A few days later, just after Dad got home from work, there was a knock on the door. It was a salesman from the shed company. He was bemused to find himself in a flat above a chemist shop, with no garden other than a window box full of bright nasturtiums. Dad was also puzzled at first but must have understood the wish for a room of one's own, because not long afterwards he built a dividing wall in the bedroom I shared with my brother.

Now I have a studio in the garden. Here, I can be completely alone, totally myself. Nothing is required of me. It is a physical home for ideas and images, a place to doze and daze the day away in imaginary worlds. It is a place of symbols, a place of history, a storehouse of memories, and a place where I can distil my thoughts. I don't even have to enter the studio to feel its power; it is sometimes enough to imagine it, my sanctuary, and know that it is there, waiting for me.

Here are two other people's physical sanctuaries.

> The first sanctuary I recall was a place in the bush that surrounded our home in Khandallah. There among the trees was an old ngaio with strong roots that pushed into the ground. Between these I created a nest which I lined with dried leaves and moss. Tucking my dress into my bloomer legs, I would curl into a ball and settle down into that quiet refuge far away from the troubles in the household: that was my special retreat until my legs grew longer and I could no longer fit comfortably into my nest.
>
> DOROTHY PASCOE

> At the back, tucked in the corner, behind the feijoa tree, I have a small corrugated iron shed that I call 'The Cave'. It is my 'God Space' where I can chill out, pray, paint, journal, write poetry. The walls are covered with paintings, scribbles, scriptures. I like to get out there early in the morning before the kids are up and the business of the day kicks in, and centre on Jesus.
>
> IAN CHARLTON

Solitude is the most powerful immunisation I have against fear of existential loneliness. It is only in solitude that I can practise being alone and *not* falling into an abyss of fear and despair. Solitude gives me the opportunity to enter the spiritual sea. Solitude is also a prerequisite for my poetry. The novelist Franz Kafka said that one of the greatest joys of solitude is writing:

> Without solitude, I could not write poetry and would lose the ability to *express* my sanctuary within. Writing means revealing oneself to excess: that utmost of self-revelation and surrender, in which a human being, when

involved with others, would feel he was losing himself … Writing that springs from the surface of existence – when there is no other way and the deeper wells have dried up – is nothing, and collapses the moment a truer emotion makes that surface shake. That is why one can never be alone enough when one writes, why there can never be enough silence around one when one writes, why even night is not night enough.[104]

One of the most famous reclusive poets, Emily Dickinson, preferred to live a secluded life yet had several deep, lifelong friendships by correspondence. Her poetry is extraordinary for her gift of using simplicity and brevity to express mysterious and mystical thoughts.

There is a solitude of space,
A solitude of sea,
A solitude of death, but these
Society shall be,
Compared with that profounder site,
That polar privacy,
A Soul admitted to Itself;
Finite Infinity.

EMILY DICKINSON[105]

Some people can block out noise, rush, crowding and complexity. I am envious of them as I am so easily distracted by external stimulation. I have to exclude it. It is much easier to be silent, still, to achieve simplicity and to take things slowly when I am alone. Also, in solitude, the only distractions are those I make myself, so I can see more clearly how I manufacture them. There's no one else to blame. If I need to, I can concentrate better, be focused, intense. Solitude is a relief, warm, exciting.

I have been fortunate that in our marriage the need for solitude is understood and supported. In the course of an ordinary day, we both spend a lot of time alone. We also have times away – and at home – alone.

In letter to a young friend who wanted to be a poet, the German author Rilke described, in my view, the ideal marriage:

The point of marriage is not to create a quick commonality by tearing down all boundaries; on the contrary, a good marriage is one in which each partner appoints the other to be the guardian of his solitude, and thus they show each other the greatest possible trust. A merging of two people is an impossibility, and where it seems to exist, it is a hemming-in, a mutual consent that robs one party or both parties of their fullest freedom and development. But once the realization is accepted that even between the closest people infinite distances exist, a marvellous living side-by-side can grow up for them, if they succeed in loving the expanse between them, which gives them the possibility of always seeing each other as a whole and before an immense sky.[106]

The many benefits of solitude have been summarised by Richard Mahler, who spent three winter months alone in the mountains of northern New Mexico:

Freedom to fantasise
Development of the imagination
Cultivation of abstract thought
Heightened awareness
Healing during stress, mourning, or other trauma
Improved concentration
Access to religious, spiritual or mystical experiences
Better problem-solving abilities
Liberation from unwanted distractions
Effective pain management skills
The rich company of one's mind, body, and spirit
Expanded self-understanding[107]

One of the beautiful paradoxes of solitude is that exploring my inner world more deeply enriches my ability to connect with others. Solitude makes truth easier. Unless I know and accept my true self, I cannot know and accept others. Unless I know the depths of my own soul, I cannot be open to other souls. When I am topped up with solitude, and nourished by my interior life, then I do not need to 'put on a show' at all. When I have enough solitude, I am authentic, genuine. I *want* to see other people, I want to communicate, reach out, help, and express my love.

I called around to a friend's house after her father's funeral. She was burning all of his possessions. I saw this carving he had made at the edge of the bonfire and asked if I could have it. You can't see in this photograph, but the top is burnt. I must be silent now. Raumati, 2001.

resonance of silence

Quietness

Inside this new love, die.
Your way begins on the other side.
Become the sky.
Take an axe to the prison wall.
Escape.
Walk out like somebody suddenly born into colour.
Do it now.
You're covered with thick cloud.
Slide out the side. Die,
and be quiet. Quietness is the surest sign
that you've died.
Your old life was a frantic running
from silence.

The speechless full moon
comes out now.

JALĀL AD-DĪN MUHAMMAD RŪMĪ[108]

Silence in society

Silence can be thought of as soft, calm, gentle, but there are also many negative connotations associated with silence – being unforthcoming, taciturn, tight-lipped. Silence can be awkward and unwelcome; even a chasm that engulfs people who cannot communicate. Enforced silence, when a person is deaf in a world that hears, is terribly isolating. Not being heard is also a kind of enforced silence, as is not being understood. Such a silence can be devastating, as poet and novelist Janet Frame articulates in her poem 'The Suicides': 'they died because words they had spoken/returned always homeless to them.'[109]

Silence can be a punishment: 'the silent treatment', 'sending someone to Coventry'. Silencing people is one of the most powerful political acts. In the Middle Ages, the brank (also called the scold's bridle) was a metal mask locked over someone's head, to force them to be silent. It had a device, called a curb, that rested on the tongue to prevent ('curb') speech. Although the brank was occasionally used on men, it was a punishment almost exclusively reserved for women, who could at the time be officially accused of and censured for being 'common scolds' – nags, gossips, shrews, trouble-makers.

Noise can also be punishing. I live in a loud society in which there is enforced noise wherever I go: cafés I can't converse in, television documentaries with speech-obliterating music, phone tones and strident one-way conversations into thin air. The supermarket is full of jangling music and clattering trolleys. Even bookshops bang out music now. Waiting for an appointment at the dentist or hospital or for some doctors, I am assaulted by the blare of talkback radio or television. Libraries, once sanctuaries of silence, have become social centres, full of people crowded around computers, playing games, and chatting. They even have music playing in libraries now. It is becoming impossible to think, or have a conversation, outside home.

Fears of silence

Perhaps we are afraid of silence? Maybe it is a fear of hearing internal noise? Inside my own head, 'monkey mind' can chatter away non-stop. I like and loathe this Buddhist term for the unsettled mind, nattering, babbling, prattling, rattling inner thoughts. It makes me think of the way a monkey screams.

Sometimes external noise silences internal noise. It's that phenomenon where people turn on the radio just to have some background noise when they are alone. Maybe we think that if we make enough noise, we don't need to listen – even to ourselves. Or maybe something more frightening? Just as solitude is confused with loneliness, silence can be confused with isolation. Maybe silence (like space and solitude) signals emptiness, nothingness, and triggers primitive fears. Maybe it signals the death of everything – including the self?

Learning from others

Doris Smeaton was a Quaker Elder. She taught by example, simple in what she did and deep in who she was. She was 90 when I first met her and we often used to sit in silence, holding hands. I can hear her now. Just before we fell into silence she would say: 'We need to press the palms of our hands together gently to feel the connection.'

Doris taught me so much about the relationship between the self and the soul. 'Take the I – the ego – out of it,' she'd say. When I asked, 'How can the self take the self away?' she replied, 'By listening to silence.' She showed me that stillness holds the secret to a state of pure being, because then the spirit is free. Once, as I was leaving, I asked her what she was going to do that afternoon. She paused a long time then said, 'I will sit here, and become the garden and the grass and the blackbird.'

Mahatma Gandhi kept one day a week of silence:

> Silence has now become both a physical and spiritual necessity for me. Originally it was taken to relieve the sense of pressure. Then I wanted time for writing. After, however, I had practiced it for some time, I saw the spiritual value in it. It suddenly flashed across my mind that that was the time when I could best hold communion with God. And now I feel as though I was naturally built for silence. Silence is a great help to a seeker of truth, like myself. In the attitude of silence the soul finds the path in a clearer light, and what is elusive and deceptive resolves itself into crystal clearness. Our life is a long and arduous quest after Truth and the soul requires inward restfulness to attain its full height.[110]

Sara Maitland wrote a superb memoir, *A Book of Silence*, reflecting on her experiences when she lived alone for some months in a remote setting.[111] She wanted to explore her own spirituality, dig deeper into her writing, and enjoy the very thing she was 'falling in love with' – silence. While on retreat, she read many accounts of silence and identified 'eight distinct experiences' that seem to occur among people who expose themselves 'voluntarily to a long period of silence, for any reason whatsoever'. These can be summed up as follows:

1. An intensification of both physical and psychological sensation;
2. Disinhibition;
3. Auditory hallucinations – 'hearing voices';
4. A sense of 'givenness' or connection;
5. Experiences of great joy that feel as though they came from 'outside' themselves – a kind of connectedness with everything;
6. Boundary confusions – where the self begins and ends;
7. An exhilarating consciousness of being at risk;
8. Ineffability and bliss.[112]

Joys of silence

Some years ago, when I was in great need of silence, my brother sent me a beautiful gift of music, along with this note:

> I've made you a tape of some very quiet, still, intense piano music, played by me, which means a lot to me. When playing it, I think much of it sounds 'monastic' and it is all very haunting and meditative although there are some fairly discordant bits in it. The whole cycle of short pieces (about 30 of them, lasting nearly an hour) is somehow tinted or imbued with the sound of BELLS, with their strange overtones of harmony, and primitive, evocative undertones. They are by the Catalan composer Federico Mompou who lived to the age of 90-odd in Barcelona and died about 20 years ago; it's called *Musica Callada* which is almost untranslatable; the closest would be 'Silent Music'.
>
> ANTHONY HALSTEAD

What was so touching about this gift was that my brother not only understood my longing for the voiceless moment, the wide stretch of possibility, but also, as a classical musician, found a way to reach the silence within me through sound.

I don't *need* to be alone to experience deep silence. Sometimes it is possible to join someone in their silence, as opposed to sitting alongside them in your own silence. To be silent with someone and not intrude, to be beside someone and not disappear, these are some of the greatest acts of love I know.

Journal, April 2011

I set up a table for your 98th birthday in half light, half shade. Wine, no candles but a cornflower-blue gingham cloth the kitchen staff lent me. Homemade pikelets and apricot jam. One of your beautiful jugs, filled with leaves from that radiant tree.

The leaves – those leaves – dying, drying, now that autumn's here, arriving only yesterday. The leaves – those leaves – in this cold snap, with the sun flashing to shock us. We talked, but mostly were silent. You closed your eyes, then so did I.

Those leaves in the trees were children clapping at a concert, gulls splashing about in the sea, rain on a red tin roof turning to hailstones. Then the birds came – the tūī cackled and crackled as they cracked a joke we didn't get. They were gurgling and yodelling with the joy of flight.

Yes, we closed our eyes and were silent. Sound came of its own accord as we sat holding hands, calling back the comfort of touch.

Several years ago I used to attend a Quaker 'meeting for worship'. I first went because I had heard that it was somewhere I could find quiet companionship. We would sit, silently, as a group, for an hour. Occasionally, people were 'moved to speak', sharing what Quakers call ministry. Almost always those spoken words belonged to the silence. As William Penn once said, 'True silence is the rest of the mind, and is to the spirit what sleep is to the body, nourishment and refreshment.'[113]

At Kopua there is a period of silence after Vespers, where people stay in the church and meditate. It is the most beautiful period of the day. In his book on personal prayer, Father John Kelly, the former Abbot of Kopua, says: 'I think that the silences are not intended primarily for personal reflection. If we use them for reflection we are no longer silent interiorly. I believe that silence, especially if it is interior, is food for our spirits. It builds us up spiritually in a hidden way.' 'Meditation is a mysterious experience. Nothing seems to be happening in the depths of silence. Yet the tree is known by its fruits.'[114]

Journal, May 2003, Kopua

Here in the monastery I can rest and gather the ghosts of my past in some semblance of meaning. Silence is home; not even the wind intrudes. At meditation, at first, all I hear are stomachs churning, an intake of breath, a creaking seat. To pray with monks is a tall order at the best of times. Then everything fades. On the edge of dark, I glimpse a point of light.

Journal, July 2008

When I listen to silence, I feel the world contract into myself. I become a globe. A perfect roundness. We are all worlds circling the world. We are all globes with infinite motion and music.

Being silent alongside the silence of others is strangely powerful. Usually I stay in my own silence, but occasionally I enter what I would call a *shared silence*. Sometimes I sense a presence as if someone else, something else, is now in the room. It is as if I feel rather than see light. At those times, I feel that I am in the presence of God. I experience this as an oceanic feeling. Maybe it is the point at which we have all left the central island of self and are swimming in the same spiritual sea.

Thomas Merton wrote in *Thoughts of Solitude*: 'Words stand between silence and silence: between the silence of things and the silence of our own being. Between the silence of the world and the silence of God. When we have really met and known the world in silence, words do not separate us from the world nor from other men, nor from God, nor from ourselves because we no longer trust entirely in language to contain reality.'[115]

A contemplation on listening to silence

I have to exclude noise that catches my attention, until attention itself is quieted. Some sounds dissolve into the silence: rain on roof, tide coming in, wind in trees, bird song, purring of cat.

To get to the centre of silence I have to stop filling silence with the talking self. The circularity of self is formidable. Only when I silence the self, can silence become *listening* to silence.

How can I describe the essence of silence in words? I can't. Making words, reading words and even thinking in words all make sounds inside my head. When I am fully silent I listen to *silence*. As I write this, silent in my studio, what can I hear besides these words in my head?

The sound of this black pen on the page.

A gulp when I swallow my coffee.

Cars on the road outside. No, a bus.

Voices from the property next door. A conversation, though I cannot hear what is said.

Someone singing. Someone laughing?

Something being revved up nearby. A car? A machine?

My stomach rumbling.

Another car, perhaps a truck?

Birds. Blackbirds? No, tūī.

The friction of my hand on the page as I smooth the paper.

The window frames creaking in the wind.

A saw, far away. Or a blowfly nearby. I can't tell the difference. But all the time I am interpreting, visualising, and filling my mind with words and pictures. Taking up the space of silence with sound.

I stop writing and just sit still, and meditate …

It is half an hour later. What happened then? What can I recall?

First, I heard more things – a dog barking, footsteps on the path. Then, my own thoughts –

swirling around, in and out of focus. As long as I was *listening* to my thoughts, I couldn't silence them. When I just observed them, with detachment, they went away. At some point I listened to something else, which I can't describe. I couldn't even paint it. I will do my best with words, but they will fail me. There are layers, or many doors, to go through.

Early on in the experience of meditation, I am conscious of approaching 'less conscious'. It's a kind of swimming in my head, sometimes a spinning sensation. I also have a sense of seeing even though my eyes are closed. Not that I am seeing something: but that I have become *seeing*.

The moment between inner silence and the silence of self is like a membrane that is billowing in the wind. Like the membrane of my ear vibrating with sounds, this membrane vibrates with breath. Being in this moment is like being on a threshold where I move in and out of fractional seconds of consciousness and unconsciousness.

Perhaps I do become unconscious; perhaps it is a kind of sleep? Maybe my soul leaves my body when I finally cross the threshold. I want to say phrases like 'reunites with its source of creation'. Maybe it is inspired again and brings back inspirations to the self. But I am labelling again, giving an *explanation*. All I know is that as I come out of the deepest silence, my breathing changes. It is almost as if I have stopped breathing and then taken a huge intake of breath, filling my whole body.

All I can say is that yes, during these experiences, I have left myself and gone elsewhere. If I look for words, I can find labels like 'the universe', 'a presence', 'God'. But all I *really* know is that I came back from the silence full, warm, calm and refreshed.

A wordless day

Imagine a day where the world agrees to silence from sunrise to sunset. Imagine getting up on such a morning to the hush, knowing that no one is speaking anywhere in the world, knowing that you are part of a connected, silent community. You touch someone to get their attention. You look into each other's eyes to read needs, intentions, feelings. You communicate the essentials; the trivial disappears. You sit and listen to silence together, as if it were music. You hear each other in ways you have hardly ever explored. You have given up written communication too. You have no symbols. What if you now give up signals of all kinds, even eye contact and touch? Would you eventually communicate by intuition alone? Would you eventually find ways to express yourself to each other more authentically than any other way we know?

There is something mesmerising about the simplicity of a red barn set in a green field. Isle of Tiree, 2001.

depth of simplicity

The more I have, the more I want.
The more I want, the less I have.
The less I have, the less I want.
The less I want, the more I have.

ANON.

Simplicity in society

Simplicity can be seen as pure, easy, straightforward, but also as dense, stupid, foolish and trivial. A simpleton is someone lacking intelligence and common sense, someone who is gullible. Such people have borne the brunt of social ridicule. Complexity is seen as somehow smarter.

When my life is too complex, my brain goes into overdrive. I get confused, and ignore the sanctuary within. The entanglement of multiplicity disconnects me from my true self.

For me, society is just too complicated. I can't process the continuous streams of information from TV, radio, papers and the internet. So much of it seems to be about directing or controlling every aspect of our lives.

Journal, January 2009

A lot of the time this year, I have been on another planet and merely pretending to be on this one. Alistair Campbell once said to me that by the time he had walked to the end of his street in Pukerua Bay he felt like he had gone abroad. This year, abroad has begun at my letterbox.

I want to understand the moon this year, and the tides, and go out at night star gazing.

There are so many levels of complexity. I imagine them like the rings of Saturn. At a daily level, the duties of life involve streams of data, scarcely information let alone facts. Not knowledge, not understanding, and certainly not wisdom.

At a national level, I so often see a chaotic and shallow world almost entirely driven by money and short-sightedness. At a global level, I see despair. The world is so out of kilter that I don't know how it can right itself. Yet most days I manage to behave as an optimist.

If we all offered the kindness of strangers, just in our own tiny local space, perhaps nationally and globally, despair would gradually dissipate and be replaced by love and hope.

We are expected to do everything at once, but one thing's for sure, it is a fallacy that we can successfully multi-task. Every few months, new cognitive research demonstrates that we are not multi-taskers. In fact, we can't handle, at any one time, more than two complicated related activities. We may think that we can, but our attention is compromised, our memory less reliable and our stress levels higher.[116]

Recently I came across a popular website called Zen Habits. The author, Leo Babauta, wrote, 'I was criticized a few weeks ago when I published 'The Simple Living Manifesto: 72 Ideas to Simplify Your Life', because many people felt the list was too long.'[117] This reminds me that humour is one of the best ways to deal with stress! He reduced his list to 10 items, advising people to tackle one a day:

1. Make a short list of the 4 or 5 most important things in your life. These are your priorities.
2. Drop one commitment – something that you really do not want to do and that doesn't do anything towards your priorities.
3. Purge a drawer. Get rid of whatever you don't use or love.
4. Set limits for things you do regularly.
5. Simplify your to do list. Make it fewer than 10 items.
6. Free up time. Wake earlier, watch less TV, disconnect from the Internet, turn off the phone, do one less thing a day.
7. Clear your desk.
8. Clear out you email inbox.
9. Move more slowly.
10. Do one thing at a time.

Some of my friends would say, 'You don't need a list, just get on with your life.' Others would say, 'There are too many lists already.' Doug would stare at such a list, bemused by the need to say anything at all about simplicity. Then he would shrug his shoulders and amble away, like Winnie the Pooh, humming. How I long to be like him!

Fears of simplicity

If I were to complete everything on the Zen Habits list, my life would be altogether simpler and I would have greater space within. I thought carefully about the list, to see if I could work out why I find simplicity so hard. Two things in particular challenge me: moving more slowly (which I will discuss in the next chapter) and getting rid of what I don't use or love.

Purging a drawer is hard enough; the idea of purging my life of what I no longer need or use takes my breath away. Yet pruning encourages growth. The awful truth is that if I can't get rid of things I no longer need or use then I am *possessed by possessions*.

A contemplation on letting go

Why do I have more than I need, hold on to things I never use, and fill my life with clutter? My immediate response is that I haven't got time to sort it out and in any case I can't decide what to keep. There's no point getting help – I'm the only person who can deal with this stuff. Mmmm … only person? For now, I'll ignore that thought …

Maybe it's fear of *not having*?
Mum never threw anything away. After a childhood of poverty, she didn't like to waste things. If she had no use for something, she would put it out in the ginnel on the cobblestones. She'd say, '*Some*one's bound to want it.' And she was right. Everything disappeared. Doug never throws anything away either. Is it because he was born in the Depression years? Did he too acquire an ethic of not wasting things? I don't think this is the reason for me as I have never experienced or feared true material deprivation.

Maybe it's a fear of *relationship*?
If I'm secure in having what I need at home, do I have less need to relate to the world? Does it mean I don't have to take the risk of relating to others? Are mementos surrogate companions?

Maybe it's a fear of *emptiness*?
Do I surround myself with possessions as a kind of insulation against emptiness in life?

Maybe it's fear of *not being*?
Do I cling on to possessions as a way of holding on to life? I've collected antique china from second-hand shops since I was about 10. Sometimes I wonder what will happen to 'my treasures' when I die. Will anyone else want them, or will they just end up back in a second-hand shop for someone like me to find? Come to think of it, that's quite a nice thought.

Richard Mahler, who experienced seclusion in the wilderness, asked himself how he might maintain the simplicity he discovered there, once he returned home.[118] His list included another challenging item for me: saying 'no' to new demands.

This is the key to why my own life is so complex! Not only do I find it difficult to say no to others, I find it difficult to say no to myself, to the part of me that thinks I must be perfect. Now what was that thing I didn't want to think about? Ah, yes, 'the only person who can do this'. What arrogance! And what arrogance to imagine I can be perfect! I continued the contemplation …

Maybe it's a fear of *losing control*?
Maybe I look in control when I'm busy but I am often perilously close to chaos. Perhaps I feel important being busy. I'm needed. My presence matters. My help to others is of value. It's a very short step to thinking I'm indispensable. When I'm rushing around, in a vortex of activity, I am the centre of my world. The centre of *the* world?

I see how much I define myself in terms of what I do and what others think of me, rather than in terms of who I am and what I think of myself. I see how I avoid noticing things, such as my true feelings – and those of others.

An underlying characteristic of not being able to let go is grandiosity – the absence of humility. It is acting as if I were in control of every aspect of my life, as if I were omnipotent. Unless I genuinely accept and love myself with all my imperfections, and all my powerlessness, life will never be simple.

This is at the heart of simplicity – becoming real. If I live my life reacting to extraneous demands and imposed ideas, then I am just churning the waves, afraid I will drown at high tide. Moreover I will use a huge amount of energy to very little purpose. If I simplify my life and give up the inner drive to do everything, then I am aware of the tides within myself and can swim.

Learning from others

Simplicity is a virtue in most spiritual traditions. Quakers, for example, believe the spiritual life is far more important than material possessions, and that by living simply a person can focus on what is important in their life.

In *Quaker Faith and Practice* it says, 'At the heart of Quaker ethics is the word "simplicity". Simplicity is forgetfulness of self and remembrance of our humble status as waiting servants of God. Outwardly, simplicity is shunning superfluities of dress, speech, behaviour and possessions, all of which tend to obscure our vision of reality. Inwardly, simplicity is spiritual detachment from the things of this world as part of the effort to fulfil the first commandment: to love God with all of the heart and mind and strength.'[119]

At Kopua, the monk's round takes him through the rhythms of the day, and requires a great deal of personal discipline. Esther de Waal has written extensively on *The Rule of Saint Benedict* and in particular on Thomas Merton. She explains that 'The Rule is also concerned to show, through the daily pattern of life which it establishes, how the monk is both to submit to time and simultaneously to transcend it.'[120]

When I am at the monastery, I join in the round as much as I can because it is so soothing. I have seen the monks greatly stretched by the work they do as part of their vocation, yet they seem able to remain calm as they continuously circle their 'round'. The monks belong to an order, in every sense. Seven times a day, at appointed hours, they gather to pray. There's no such thing as a chaos of monks.

Journal, March 2004, Kopua

The shape of the day is better here. It curves on itself, like a natural circle. All I have to do is step on the rim to be carried from morning till night.

To stay, to pray in the present. To be grateful for the smallest thing. To see breath as a gift. That's the answer.

Faith is easier in this place. Maybe it's the chanting monks in the morning sun, the constant wind in the trees, the boundless view. You.

There are so many reminders of spiritual life in the day-to-day round at Kopua. The Angelus is rung to remind the monks to stand still for a moment and remember the annunciation. Just before bedtime, at the office of Compline, the Abbot sprinkles holy water on people as they leave the church. I am told it is a reminder of baptism.

Religious rituals and routines are both ways and reminders to stay connected with God. I remember hearing the muezzin calling from the mosque in Agra, reminding Muslims to 'hasten to prayer'. This happens five times a day – at dawn, midday, the middle of the afternoon, just after sunset, and about two hours after sunset.

The word for the Hebrew Prayer Book is *Siddur*. The ritual meal at *Pesach* (Passover) is called the *Seder*. Both *Siddur and Seder* come from a Hebrew root meaning order, as in order of events. In Judaism there are many *mitzvot,* or religious duties, such as regular prayers and blessings, washing of hands, lighting of candles and so on. The word *mitzvot* means commands or commandments. The word *mitzvah* (the singular form) also means connection, and in some Jewish writings is seen to assign a higher function to the *mitzvah*: to enhance through ritual the connection between the human being and God.[121]

Rituals embody both order and significance. They can hold back our fear of formlessness as we express our deepest emotions – love, fear, grief. The oldest rituals often involve the stars and planets, most notably the sun and moon, because they are deeply related to our relationship with time and nature. The primitive elements – water, air, earth, fire – are nearly always a part of ritual, because they are deeply related to our experience of space and survival. The rituals of my childhood connect me to some of the deepest truths in my soul.

Joys of simplicity

When things are simpler I see patterns more clearly, I am calmer, life is better, more meaningful, and my personal relationships are richer. For me, the joys of simplicity include:

Caring for myself as well as others

My wish is to care for others but to do so I have to care for myself first. This does not come naturally to me, so I have to do this very consciously. In the distance, beyond some horizon I may never even get close to, there is a space where selflessness embodies everything. Where there is no need for a barrier between self and others. Now, I still to need to withdraw to consciously take care of myself or else I get overwhelmed, then ill. At my weakest, I create huge walls to make sure that I will not be overwhelmed by closeness. At my strongest, I can take down those walls and let people in. Then, I can enter life and *become*. This means quite simply having enough exercise, nutrition, rest, sleep, company and space for my soul. It also means remembering to take my medications and having the humility to ask for help from others when I need it.

Knowing the difference between want and need

I need air, water, food, warmth, shelter and love to survive. All else is optional. I might want a new printer, a pair of red boots, enough coloured pens, more bluebells, a week in Paris, a month in Antarctica, but I'll survive without them. I write down daily the things for which I am grateful. It leads to a state of grace.

Being as willing to receive as to give

It's easier to give than to receive. Perhaps that is because there can be issues of power connected with giving and receiving. To receive means being open, and that can mean being vulnerable. That requires humility. I have noticed that when I need something, it seems to appear in my life, as long as I am in a state of receptiveness.

Having humility

The Buddhist ideal of not being driven by desire; the Christian ideal of selfless love; the Jewish ideal of *bittel* or humility; the Islamic idea of '*Inshallah*!' or 'If Allah wills' all point to the same conclusion. All I can do is to be prepared and willing to do my best: the rest is up to God. And I know that given the same opportunities that I have had, other people may have done far more of value.

Having routines in my life

Learning from the monks at Kopua, I have developed my own daily round: Prayer, Walk, Meditation, Work, Rest, Work, Relaxation, Prayer. When I follow these daily practices I feel more balanced. They comfort me and make my connection to my soul stronger.

Having rituals in my life

I have many rituals in my life, small and large, regular and rare. Many of those rituals are spiritual. Sometimes we need to create our own rituals.

When my friend Betty died in 2002 I was unable to be in Scotland for her funeral. I needed some ritual here in New Zealand. I invited 11 women friends to a ceremony, in the garden at home. We sang the hymns sung at her funeral and a friend sang 'Mary of Argyll' – the song Alex had sung to Betty when he proposed to her. The meal consisted of all Betty's favourite foods, and was served on antique dishes because she and I shared a great love of antique china. Twelve women sat in a circle and read her poems and talked of the meaning of friendship. I dedicated an area of the garden to her, and we each planted a Christmas lily there.

Similarly, when my mother died in 2006 in England I had not long returned to New Zealand after visiting her, and could not go back again so soon. Instead, I went to Kopua and there at exactly the same time as her funeral service in Manchester I went into the church – it was late at night here

– and lit a candle for her and read aloud the same funeral service, said the same psalms and sang the same hymns. I was here in New Zealand as my brother was there in England and there was no distance between us.

Concentrating on what matters most

To do this means knowing my priorities. At the beginning of a new year I like to think about my life and what is possible. I want to focus on positive things, the things that give meaning to my life. So I identify some meaningful goals. Then I write down actions that will help me to achieve each goal. It is very important to see the difference between what I can control and what I cannot. All I can control is my *preparedness* and *willingness* to achieve what I believe matters in life.

Meaningful goals for 2011

Listen to my soul
Express my love
Have authentic relationships
Write what matters most
Educate myself
Have fun
Look after my health
Look after our home
Have order in my life
Handle my worries well
Leave space for opportunities
Be simple. Be silly.

Being silly

We can sometimes be at our happiest and most hopeful when we are being silly, yet the 'biography' of the word silly reads like a psychological thriller. Originally silly meant happy, prosperous, blessed, from the Old English word *gesælig*. By the twelfth century it meant pious and innocent. By the later thirteenth century it meant pitiable. Then it came to mean weak and by end of the sixteenth century it meant feeble in mind, lacking in reason, foolish and simple.[122]

Ernest, my mother's youngest brother, was labelled a simpleton at school. Throughout his life he put up with people treating him as someone who was 'a penny short of a shilling'. He was one of the gentlest, kindest people I have ever known. He was greatly loved by those who knew him. Like my grandfather James, he had very poor eyesight and gradually became blind. I have so many loving memories of Uncle Ernie. He was childlike and brought out the child in me. We shared a love of tigers and once, when one escaped from a zoo in England, we waved and cheered it on as we listened to the radio reports of its progress.

This 'simple' man would occasionally come out with the most profound comment as if he'd just plucked it from the air:

A mild-mannered man

To get its sense, draw
close and open a curtain
onto the kitchen where
my Uncle Ernie sits
hand in hand
with himself.

His shirt done up to
the collar bone.
His braces covered by
a thin blue gansie.
As my Dad would say.

He calls me love
and makes me feel
at home 12,000
miles away.

When I last visited
he casually mentioned
(over tea) that time
is infinite. He'd heard
it somewhere and felt
the truth of it.

He continued to stir
the pot and quietly
explain that
it took longer to get
from here to there
than there to here

because here to there is further.[123]

One of the things I do to slow my mind down is walk. It's like getting a brain massage. When I walk on the beach at sunset, I see the gulls flying back to Kapiti Island. It's as if they are reminding me: 'Hey look! It's time to rest now.' Raumati, 2006.

quick of slowness

Whether you are going too fast and your life is unmanageable, or not – at the root of all our psychological problems lies a busy mind, trapped by its own thinking.

JOSEPH BAILEY[124]

Slowness in society

Slowness may be associated with being measured, deliberate, considered and unhurried but it is also often linked to being stupid, dull, sluggish and dawdling. A child with learning difficulties used to be called 'slow'. We associate slowing down with old age and retirement from life. Some of the crises in society are when the economy 'slows down', when business is slow, or when workers are on a 'go slow'.

Modern Western culture idolises speed. We treat deadlines as if they were lifelines. In his book *In Praise of Slowness: How a worldwide movement is challenging the cult of speed,* Carl Honoré says we are becoming *addicted* to speed and that fast and slow are shorthand for ways we live our life.[125] He considers that they imply far more than a rate of movement: living in a fast way is often tied up with control and superficiality whereas living life slowly is more about being aware and noticing the connections between things.

One of the ways we have increased the speed of everyday life is the development of digital technology, which itself is built on the premise that speed is of utmost importance. How quickly can we download? How fast is the response? Speed gives an illusion of control.

In *The Shallows: How the internet is changing the way we think, read and remember*, Nicholas Carr argues that the Internet has altered an 'intellectual ethic', which he defines as the message that a medium or other tool transmits into the minds and culture of its users. For instance, every single development in writing technology has influenced the content of what is written.[126]

It has long been recognised that every shift in the development of human cognitive skills brings a shift in 'intellectual ethic'. In *Phaedrus*, discussing the developing use of the written word, Plato has Socrates argue that writing itself will reduce memory, and therefore wisdom.[127]

It may well be that we are adapting to the technological shift in valuable ways, but there are costs. Carr calls the web 'a technology of forgetfulness'. There is abundant, convincing research that shows that people who use the Internet regularly and extensively are 'rewiring' their brains to search for and use knowledge in ways consistent with the design of the internet itself. 'Just as neurons that fire together, wire together, neurons that don't fire together, don't wire together.'[128]

The goal of speed is changing the way we read. Speed reading was once thought to be a rare skill, now it is the norm when using a computer. We scan rather than read, highlight rather than take notes, snip rather than join up and, most dangerously, we are constantly reading things out of their context.

I enjoy my computer and recognise the many ways it has enhanced my life but I am shot down by these bullet points:

- The more I use a system that divides my attention, distracts me and interrupts what I am doing, the less I concentrate and focus.
- The more I use a system with the primary design goal of speed, the less able I am to go slowly.
- The more I use search techniques that encourage me to pursue breadth and multiple, often tenuous, connections, the less I concentrate in depth on the relationship between ideas.
- The more I rely on a computer to remember things for me, the less I store, which means the less I synthesise in my own memory.
- The more time I spend in a world of mental noise, the less I experience mental silence.
- The more I experience information overload, the less space I have for creative thinking.

Fears of slowness

Most of my life I've only had two speeds: full steam ahead and crash. Sometimes I speed up without any reason at all. I just seem to 'rev up'. I might rush into the kitchen to get the evening meal on, fling things into saucepans and make a terrible mess as I go, of potato peelings and whatever else I am hurriedly preparing. It's not uncommon for me to burn a sauce or spill something on the bench and at those times I am often trying to do too many things at the same time: catch the news, feed the cats, send an email, stir the casserole, put the car away, check the vegetables, and, if I have been foolish enough to leave off the answer-machine, maybe even pick up the phone when it rings, all the while getting more het-up.

This scenario sounds crazy. It *is*. It is about feeling out of control within and trying to become calmer by controlling things outside myself – a strategy that almost always fails. Maybe we are afraid that we won't do everything we want to in our life. Maybe being addicted to speed is a conviction that if we go fast enough we will fit as much as possible into the life we are given? Speed is always a race against some measure of time. It is as if we think we can win against time itself if we only go fast enough. Is this what fear of slowness is about?

I sense something deeper, even atavistic here: fear of being left behind by one's tribe, fear of not having food and shelter, fear of not being able to flee the foe. To be quick originally meant 'to be alive'. I wonder if we even associate slowness with dying? I wonder if fear of slowness is actually fear of death?

Learning from others

Clearly it is hard to be slow when bringing up a family, juggling jobs and being involved in the local community. Slowness is obviously easier when you have less to do. Yet, to some extent, slowness begins inside. In *The Speed Trap*, Joseph Bailey says that our personal world, the world of our psychological experience of life, is created from the *inside* out.[129]

Someone I met at Kopua told me he slowed down his inner self through the sanctuary of nature:

> I like to get away from all things made by human hands – concrete, steel, glass, wood etc. – and be surrounded by God's creation, whether it's a beautiful stream, bush or some lonely beach. It helps to melt away the hectic city life and connect with creation's rhythm. The tides, swells, flow of streams, trees swaying in the breeze ... I feel my inner self slow down till I reach God's rhythm again, and I gain an immense sense of peace and quiet in my soul. My eyes begin to see God afresh and He speaks to me through His creation. I hear the words I need to hear. Once a week I try to get out into nature – it could be to surf, fish a stream, head into the bush or to crash up a mountainside.
>
> IAN CHARLTON

There is increasing interest in the idea of being slow as a way of life; a phenomenon sometimes called 'the Slow movement'. There are books in abundance about the art of being slow: slow in life generally, or specifically about slow gardening, cooking, reading, and so on. In *Slow Reading*, John Miedema writes, 'If you want the deep experience of a book, if you want to internalise it, to mix an author's ideas with your own and make it a more personal experience, you have to read it slowly.'[130]

Miedema's words recall the ancient practice *lectio divina*, which I first came across through the Quakers, and have since learnt more about through visits to Kopua. The phrase is a Latin one meaning 'divine word'. *Lectio divina* is the polar opposite of speed-reading. It is a method of reflecting so deeply on one small written passage, or even on one word, that its essential meaning becomes part of you.

When Sister Thelma Hall wrote *Too Deep for Words: Rediscovering Lectio Divina* in 1985, lectio seemed to have fallen by the wayside, although it was 'a proven path to contemplation for centuries'.[131] She describes the four stages usually identified in the process of *lectio divina*. They are *lectio*, reading and listening to the word of God; *meditatio*, meditation, reflecting on the word; *oratio*, where the word touches the heart; and *contemplatio*, contemplation, entering the silence. This fourth stage gives her book its title.

Similarly, in *Silence, Solitude, Simplicity*, Sister Jeremy Hall describes some fundamentals of 'a Benedictine way' to God. She discusses *The Rule of Saint Benedict* with its inter-related 'tools' of obedience, silence, humility and prayer, and she too includes a discussion of the practice of *lectio* – a way of reading holy writings 'so that the whole person is engaged'.[132] She refers to the first treatise on *lectio*, by Guigo II, a Carthusian Prior, who described the four stages. She interprets them as deep reading of the text; meditating on its meaning; praying in light of its meaning; and finally, being present with God in light of its meaning. She offers guidelines on how to use *lectio* in everyday life as a way of increasing receptivity to spiritual inspiration.[133]

The closest I come to using *lectio divina* is reading extremely slowly, phrase by phrase, word by word. Sometimes I stop over a word for so long that I feel it is somewhere inside me. Even if we don't know the meaning of a word, we can reflect on its shape, or even focus on a single letter. Learning Hebrew is such a joy. Each letter is not just a shape and sound but is full of meaning, a symbol of philosophy and history. According to some Talmudic mystic sources, each letter is believed to be a building block of creation.[134]

The best pace

Friends gave me the perfect present a few years ago, which I read during a long New Zealand summer, lying in the grass, pausing over words, stopping to think for as long as I needed. *The Discovery of Slowness* by Sten Nadolyn is a meditation on time and perception built into an historical fiction about Sir John Franklin. I have long been intrigued by this nineteenth-century explorer of the Arctic. So this gift related to two areas of interest – Franklin and slowness.

This book was written to be read slowly. As Nadolyn interprets Franklin's life, his central proposition is that Franklin was slow from birth: he perceives the world slowly, hears things slowly, thinks, speaks and, most importantly, makes decisions slowly. 'Now and then, John sat in front of the hut, bundled in heavy clothing, looking at an autumn storm sweeping swarms of the last leaves off the branches. John picked out a specific leaf and waited for it to fall. Often this allowed him many hours of aimless and unhurried contemplation.'[135]

People thought that John Franklin was stupid. They made fun of him for being so slow. They thought he was incapable of making decisions because he took his time. Yet John recognised when events called for speed and delegated as necessary. Maybe what matters is finding the right pace.

Pace alters perspective. When I go fast I only see the big picture, the main features, the gist. When I go slowly I only see specific images, details, parts of the whole. Carl Honoré says, 'The Slow philosophy can be summed up in a single word: balance. Be fast when it makes sense to be fast, and be slow when slowness is called for. Seek to live at what musicians call the *tempo giusto* – the right speed.'[136]

Maybe, like Franklin, many of us have a natural pace, a unique rhythm. When I do manage to slow down I often experience a strong physical release – the long breath out. As I have become older and been able to explore slowness more, I have come to think that being slow is my natural state and I have been behaving *how I thought I had to* most of my life. A sobering thought.

Joys of slowness

Earlier I described the crazy scene of rushing around the kitchen on a night when I am chasing imaginary deadlines. Now on another night, for reasons I do not know, I find myself staring out of the window by the kitchen bench …

Red geraniums in terracotta pots. A suggestion of sunset in the clouds. Slowly I prepare the carrots, studying the depth of colour, then I stroll out to the compost bin with wafer-thin slivers of peel in my hands.

A cat sidles by, his tail in a question mark. He squeezes himself under the gate into the garden sanctuary – he knows this is where we always cuddle. We sit at the table, under the walnut tree, and smooch for a while – my face smoothing his fur.

Meanwhile the six o'clock news may have come and gone but I have watched gum trees wavering in the wind and I have seen the scarlet clouds of sunset.

The scent of wood smoke lures me back inside. The fire is blazing and Doug has clinched the last clue of the crossword. I think to myself – 'I'll make those salmon fishcakes that he loves.' So I step out again, to pick parsley, and I notice the edge of Scorpio rising.

I think the phone has rung but I ignored it. And I'm not checking emails tonight. I want to be here. There's an easy evening ahead, and that letter from Chrissie to read …

It's rare to get a handwritten letter nowadays. I love it when I find one in the box. It's an intimate experience to see a friend's handwriting and hold and smell the paper they have handled. When I receive a personal, handwritten letter I have a sense that someone has held me closely in mind. I also believe that what they say matters. The value of an idea is somehow reflected in the care that goes into its presentation.

If I want the deep experience of writing, then I write by hand. There is something so physical about writing. It is something to do with embodiment. I have a sense of wholeness – mind, body and soul – when I write poetry. When I form the letters by hand, I am more connected to what I am saying. I can *feel* the words better as they travel from my heart, through my head, down my arm, onto the page.

Similarly, when I read poems slowly and aloud, rather than silently, my experience of them is much more physical and I am far more affected by them.

Six poems to read slowly

GERRIT ACHTERBERG (1905–1962)

Snow Passage

Since it so quietly began to snow,
new distances have awakened within me.
I would like to go to every person now
and say: I wasn't like you had thought;
perhaps they didn't feel pity for me;
they have their own pursuits.
The darkness lessens, the trees
are turning whiter around me.
One remains there standing in the loneliness,
and desire and tears pass away, its steps
disappear in the snow, at the end of the night
awaits the white morning, showered in sunlight.

Translated from the Dutch by Cliff Crego[137]

WISLAWA SZYMBORSKA (1923–2012)

A Note

Life is the only way
to get covered in leaves,
catch your breath on the sand,
rise on wings;

to be a dog,
or stroke its warm fur;

to tell pain
from everything it's not;

to squeeze inside events,
dawdle in views,
to seek the least of all possible mistakes.

An extraordinary chance
to remember for a moment
a conversation held
with the lamp switched off;

and if only once
to stumble upon a stone,
end up soaked in one downpour or another,

mislay your keys in the grass;
and to follow a spark on the wind with your eyes;
and to keep on not knowing
something important.

Translated from the Polish by Stanislaw Baranczak and Clare Cavanagh[138]

To Everything There is a Season

To every thing there is a season, and a time to every purpose under the heaven:

A time to be born, and a time to die; a time to plant, and a time to pluck up that which is planted;

A time to kill, and a time to heal; a time to break down, and a time to build up;

A time to weep, and a time to laugh; a time to mourn, and a time to dance;

A time to cast away stones, and a time to gather stones together; a time to embrace, and a time to refrain from embracing;

A time to get, and a time to lose; a time to keep, and a time to cast away;

A time to rend, and a time to sew; a time to keep silence, and a time to speak;

A time to love, and a time to hate; a time of war, and a time of peace.

What profit hath he that worketh in that wherein he laboureth?

I have seen the travail, which God hath given to the sons of men to be exercised in it.

He hath made every thing beautiful in his time: also he hath set the world in their heart, so that no man can find out the work that God maketh from the beginning to the end.

I know that there is no good in them, but for a man to rejoice, and to do good in his life.

And also that every man should eat and drink, and enjoy the good of all his labour, it is the gift of God.

I know that, whatsoever God doeth, it shall be for ever: nothing can be put to it, nor any thing taken from it: and God doeth it, that men should fear before him.

That which hath been is now; and that which is to be hath already been; and God requireth that which is past.

ECCLESIASTES 3:1–15
(King James Version)

YEHUDA AMICHAI (1924–2000)

A Man in His Life

A man doesn't have time in his life
to have time for everything.
He doesn't have seasons enough to have
a season for every purpose. Ecclesiastes
was wrong about that.

A man needs to love and to hate at the same moment,
to laugh and cry with the same eyes,
with the same hands to throw stones and to gather them,
to make love in war and war in love.
And to hate and forgive and remember and forget,
to arrange and confuse, to eat and to digest
what history
takes years and years to do.

A man doesn't have time.
When he loses he seeks, when he finds
he forgets, when he forgets he loves, when he loves
he begins to forget.

And his soul is seasoned, his soul
is very professional.
Only his body remains forever
an amateur. It tries and it misses,
gets muddled, doesn't learn a thing,
drunk and blind in its pleasures
and its pains.

He will die as figs die in autumn,
Shrivelled and full of himself and sweet,
the leaves growing dry on the ground,
the bare branches pointing to the place
where there's time for everything.

Translated from the Hebrew by Chana Bloch and Stephen Mitchell[139]

RABINDRANATH TAGORE (1861–1941)

Gitanjali Verse 12

The time that my journey takes is long and the way of it long.

I came out on the chariot of the first gleam of light, and pursued my voyage through the wildernesses of worlds leaving my track on many a star and planet.

It is the most distant course that comes nearest to thyself, and that training is the most intricate which leads to the utter simplicity of a tune.

The traveller has to knock at every alien door to come to his own, and one has to wander through all the outer worlds to reach the innermost shrine at the end.

My eyes strayed far and wide before I shut them and said 'Here art thou!'

The question and the cry 'Oh, where?' Melt into tears of a thousand streams and deluge the world with the blood of the assurance 'I am!'[141]

BRIAN TURNER (1944–)

Sliding By

The river's not so solitary
the way you're turning out to be

and maybe it's better at life.
You've been walking

down by the river, you've
been talking to the wide river,

you've been observing
the rivers of sky in the river

running by, and bye and bye
is what time says to you

and the river sliding by
sly as sly. And when you

step in the river and go
to cross to the other side

you pause half way
and the water piles high

against your thigh
as you wonder whether

to go forward or back
where you've been, what you had.[141]

How to be still? Watch a cat at rest. Raumati, 2012.

quiver of stillness

You do not need to leave your room.
Remain sitting at your table and listen.
You need not even listen; simply wait.
You need not even wait, just learn to become quiet and still, and solitary,
The world will freely offer itself to you
to be unmasked.
It has no choice.
It will roll in ecstasy at your feet.

FRANZ KAFKA[142]

Stillness in society

Society is as ambivalent about stillness as it is about space, solitude, silence, slowness and simplicity. Stillness can be seen as calm, tranquil, restful, but there are many negative connotations: static, inert, stagnant. It can also be seen as lazy, passive, idle and indecisive.

Enforced stillness, like enforced solitude and silence, can be a punishment. Philippe Pinel removed the shackles from his patients in the lunatic asylum in 1794, yet physical restraints are still commonplace in psychiatric hospitals. Straitjackets, locked rooms, compulsory medication, rapid and long-term sedation are used even though there is a high risk of injury associated with such procedures. Enforced stillness, by medication and restraint, is also common in rest homes for elderly people.

Is the maddening stress of crowds, noise, complication and hurry a modern phenomenon? Is it a result of technology and rampant consumerism? The chronic nagging voice inside, the crushing urgency, physical tension and fear are not new to the world. Here's what William Penn said in the late 1600s:

> And till we are persuaded to stop, and step a little aside, out of the noisy Crowd and Incumbering Hurry of the World, and Calmly take a Prospect of Things, it will be impossible we should be able to make a right Judgement of our Selves or know our own Misery. But after we have made the just Reckonings which Retirement will help us to, we shall begin to think the World is in great measure Mad, and that we have been in a sort of Bedlam all this while.[143]

There has always been a need to step away from the crowd, step back and step within oneself. Haste so quickly becomes panic. All those breathless words – hurried, harried, harassed, hassled – become those scratchy words – jittery, jumpy, twitchy, fidgety, edgy, needled, niggled. Despite my awareness of this, I can still sometimes believe that if I can just get that done, finish this, sort that out and put everything in order, then I can be still for a while. This is the wrong way around! If I just can be still for a while, then everything will come into order.

Movement rather than stillness is the most common metaphor for the development of spiritual life. Think of Dante's journeys through Hell, Purgatory and Paradise in *The Divine Comedy* or Christian's travels in Bunyan's *The Pilgrim's Progress*. A journey to Mecca is one of the five pillars of Islam. The Baal Shem Tov taught that the Israelites' 42 separate journeys from Egypt to the Promised Land represent the phases of our lives.

A journey is an exciting metaphor. The movement of journey – the activity – captures change, dynamism, being alive! It summons up images of mountains, oceans, plains, rivers, as the topography of the mind. It evokes directions, landmarks and obstacles. We envisage starting points, crossroads, distances and various ways to travel. We conjure up navigation, adventure, exploration, discovery and the quest to reveal the unknown.

Yet the metaphor of a journey can also summon up fear, if it is a journey of migration or of exile. There will be loss of home, family, community and the familiar. Such journeys can even steal one's identity.

Even when a journey is a vacation, it can be very stressful before you even leave home. You might make plans for which way to travel and where to stay. You might take provisions, maps, guidebooks, special clothes. You may need to learn a foreign language, cancel the papers, or put the cat in the cattery. You mustn't forget your passport and tickets and have you changed some money?

The metaphor of a journey for spiritual growth has never fitted my own experience. I have not found revelation through exploration. I have learned in stillness that every spiritual revelation that I have had has found me.

Fears of stillness

Stillness is in some ways a detachment from what we have come to see as life. A stillborn child does not live. A still life painting often features dead animals. Symbols of death are of cold, immutable, still – gravestones, tombs, obelisks. Are we uncomfortable with stillness because it suggests our own mortality?

I am not afraid of my death, but I am certainly afraid of *how* I might die. And I am afraid of facing the death of people I love. There isn't a day when I don't think about death. That may sound morbid, macabre. Yet to be aware of death also enhances life.

Let me think about the closest I have come to death and what I have learnt about that through stillness. I used to see depression as a wolf at the door and I had to keep the door barred all the time. I would use all my energy barricading my house to stop the wolf coming in. But it would sniff at the windows, howl down the chimney and eventually scratch its way in. By then it was hungrier than ever and I was so weak from barring the door, that I was easy to devour. The more we resist something, the more it attracts and even possesses us. Sometimes it is better to give in. In the case of depression, that meant learning a lot about wolves and how to befriend them. I have *had* to learn how to transcend the suffering of depression in order to transform it.

I used to think that depression was an absence of energy: a void, a numbness, paralysis. I now know that energy is *trapped* by depression. I might even say that depression is trapped energy. I have to find ways to release that energy. Strangely, standing still (giving up the urge to keep moving as a way of avoiding emotions) can achieve that because I can begin to take care of myself properly.[144] Standing still may flood me with pain at first but eventually it floods me with relief. The more I practise being still, the more open I become to my deep, even raw, emotions. Then they can be transformed into energy.

I let thoughts inhabit my mind. A better habit is meditation. The word comes from Latin *meditari*, meaning to think over. It is thought to be connected to the word *mederi*, meaning to heal. To meditate is to think over and heal.

There are many kinds of meditation but basically it is a technique for clearing the mind of thoughts and being still within oneself. It might be used for relaxation or as a way of entering a state of altered consciousness, or as prayer, or for any number of personal reasons. I use a version of transcendental meditation, which I practise once a day (ideally twice a day). There are some days when I can't clear thoughts at all, but most of the time it works and sometimes I even enter 'the space inside the heart'. Sometimes there's no emotion attached to the meditation at all. At other times tears run down my face. Not tears of sadness or joy. I don't know – just tears.

Learning from others

I learned a lot about agitation and stillness from my parents. Mum was an active, energetic woman, always on the go. I can see her now, even when she sat down to read or rest, she jigged her feet and tapped her fingers. Only now when I am older can I begin to understand where her agitation came from. My mother was very intelligent – a capable woman, with an extremely active mind. She had longed to stay at school and dreamed of going to university but left school at 14 to become a factory machinist. Such was the context of her generation and social circumstances. Later, the chores of being 'housewife and mother' in the 1950s were endless. I think she was full of unexpressed intellectual and emotional energy. She was never without a book and her beloved dictionary and thesaurus were thumbed into shreds. But nothing filled her deepest longings.

Dad, on the other hand, loved being still. He too was very hard working, with a job during the day and a second job two nights a week. He enjoyed working on the house, decorating and improving things, but he also loved sitting in his armchair and gazing into the fire. And I loved watching him. There is something calming about being around a calm person.

Doug reminds me of my father in this respect. He does things slowly and thoroughly. Stillness is his way to tranquillity and serenity. I watch him sitting in one place, motionless, staring out of a window, for an hour or more. I wonder what he is thinking or if he is so far away in the clouds that language no longer exists.

In his work *Personal Prayer,* Father John Kelly of Southern Star Abbey explains how the words contemplation and prayer are used interchangeably with meditation and how these have words changed over time.[145] He defines prayer in the words of St Theresa of Avila, as 'communion with one whom we know loves us'. After reflecting on what is known about how Jesus prayed, he identifies three kinds of prayer: public worship, prayer relating to a specific action, and solitary prayer. He says this third kind of prayer is not shaped by others, or by a known or habitual form. It is something we discover through a wish to commune deeply with God. This is what Father Kelly describes as mediation – a means of entering into deep silence and stillness, and in this manner honouring our longing to be close to God.

When I was young, I used to think of prayer as asking God for something I wanted. Maybe it is more about listening to what God wants. Sometimes I pray by meditation, but also by gardening, listening to music, walking on the beach. Sometimes, prayer is putting flowers on the table ready for the *Shabbat* meal or lighting candles. It might be writing a thank you letter to God. It might be sitting in silence with a friend, or holding Doug's hand in the night. In *Modeh Ani*, the Morning Prayer, I thank God for mercifully restoring my soul within me, and showing great faithfulness.

The practice of meditation is known in all spiritual traditions, with perhaps the best-known forms being in early Buddhist and Hindu traditions. Meditation is also a spiritual practice in the Sufi (mystical) tradition of Islam. Only now am I beginning to study Jewish meditation and turning to the books of Rabbi Aryeh Kaplan.[146] Les Lancaster, a Professor of Transpersonal Psychology, also gives an accessible modern summary in his books.[147]

I first met the early English mystics when I was studying the wondrous Old English texts such as *The Wanderer* and *The Seafarer* and those Middle English texts like *Ancrene Wisse* and *Piers Plowman.*[148] When I read these works, in my early twenties, my focus was on how to translate them in order to pass exams rather than on their deeper meaning. It was to be many years before I began to appreciate the ideas they contained. By then, I had visited Kopua for the first time and come across other mystics. I was introduced to St John of the Cross, who wrote breathtaking poetry,[149] and St Teresa of Avila who explored *The Interior Castle*.[150] I met Julian of Norwich, a fourteenth-century English mystic, who shared her revelations about divine love with crystal simplicity.[151] Best of all, I found *The Cloud of Unknowing*, to me the most intriguing of the mediaeval mystical texts I have read.[152]

Joys of stillness

A friend with whom I share a love of poetry called by the house one day when I was out. The next day he sent his reply to my question about sanctuary:

> As one matures, one takes on responsibilities and having a sanctum becomes more difficult. When driving my car I sometimes see an uncomplicated green paddock and I yearn to leave my car, climb the fence and sit and enjoy the tranquillity of such a sanctuary. This did happen for me once when going around Lake Taupo. I pulled off the road, walked through a small area of bush and sat down by the edge of the lake – a sanctum indeed.
>
> As recently as midday yesterday, when I called to see you, I knocked on the door and found there was no one home. I experienced a wonderful feeling of calm. Your front porch became a sanctuary. I looked through the door and saw several crosswords on the table, and a basket of walnuts in the porch seemed to add to the charm of the place. I had found a refuge and was temporarily insulated against day-to-day cares and worries.
>
> BRIAN MEXTED

Stillness of mind is crucial for a writer. Being still gives me focus, balance, acceptance, equanimity. Most importantly, when I am still, not moving, I am *moved*.

Journal, July 2008, Kopua

When I am still, I can be in timeless spacelessness. Not future, not past, not even here. But where time doesn't even matter. Where space is not even a concept. I am alive.

I don't think that death is timeless. I think that being is timeless.

I am trying to describe an experience where space is non-space, where dark and light cease to be different, where music and silence are the same, where stillness is motion, and where solitude is connection.

This is sanctuary. It is the essence of being. The being of being.

In a cherished book, *Becoming a Writer*, Dorothea Brande describes 'the artistic coma' and how to induce it. She is talking about stilling the mind to tap into the unconscious mind in order to write:

> Learn to hold your mind as still as your body … When you have succeeded, even a little, try holding a story idea, or a character, in your mind and letting your stillness centre around that. Presently you will see the almost incredible results. Ideas which you held rather academically and unconvincingly will take on colour and form; a character that was a puppet will move and breathe. Consciously or unconsciously every successful writer who ever lives calls on this faculty to put the breath of life into this creation.[153]

Journal, January 2011, Kopua

I do not feel that I am travelling at all. I am standing still. I am staying in one place and absorbing it to the extent to which I am capable. I see the same things day after day, not new faces and places. But I see them differently each day.

I am not travelling through countries. I am my own country. I am where I am and who I am. I notice and appreciate the old and familiar in every detail.

Stillness IS space. The space between one breath and another, one heartbeat and another, one blink of the eye and another.

It is the space between this word

and this.

Between dipping a brush in paint and laying it on paper.

It is the space between the birth and death of a star I will see in the sky tonight.

I want to notice these spaces because that is being – being still.

Stillness distils.

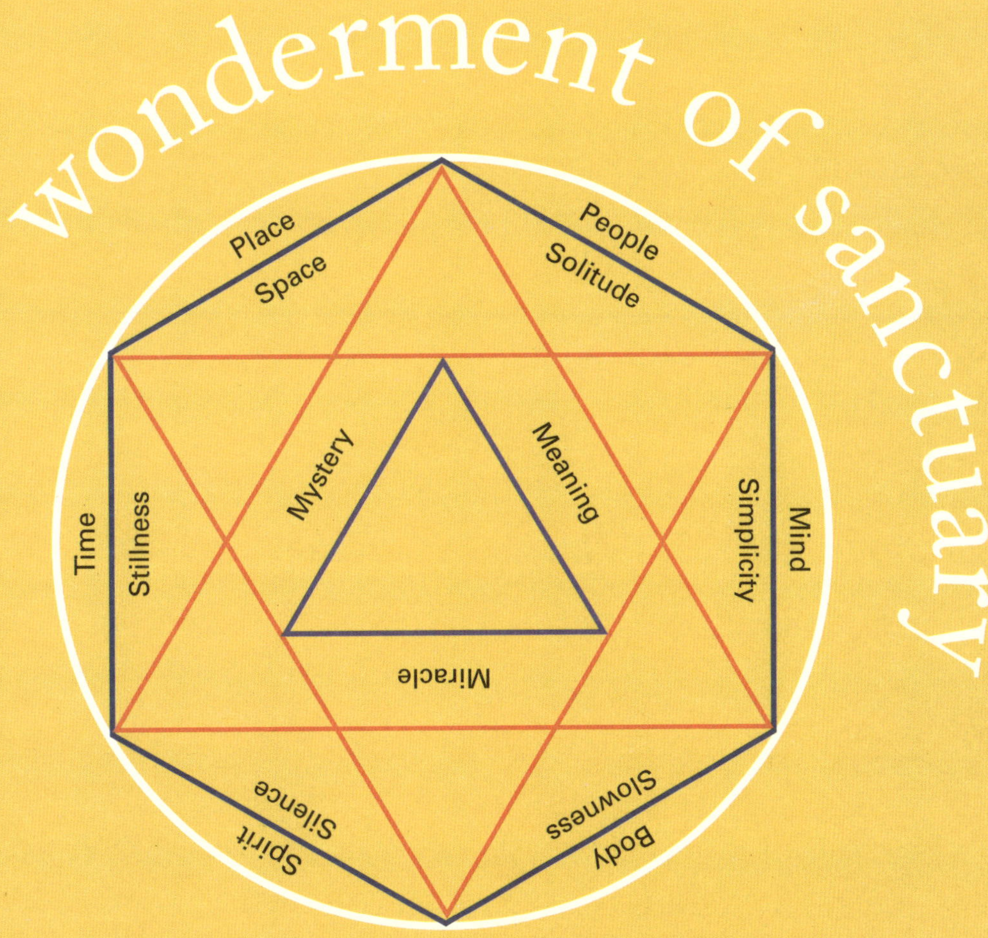
wonderment of sanctuary
Place
Space
People
Solitude
Time
Stillness
Mystery
Meaning
Simplicity
Mind
Miracle
Spirit
Silence
Slowness
Body

The early morning mist at the monastery is the perfect opening to a day there. Kopua, 2013.

mystery

> The fairest thing we can experience is the mysterious. It is the fundamental emotion which stands at the cradle of true art and true science. He who knows it not and can no longer wonder, no longer feel amazement, is as good as dead, a snuffed-out candle.
>
> ALBERT EINSTEIN[154]

Human beings want to *solve* things. People delight in brainteasers: enigmas and conundrums, quizzes and crosswords, Sudoku and pictograms. They get hooked on chess, bridge, mahjong, poker and all manner of online puzzles. Solving is a way of learning – we remember something better when we find the answers to questions ourselves.

The Vedas, *The Qur'an*, the Torah and the New Testament all teach by means of riddles. Temples in China, Tibet and Japan have puzzles engraved on the walls.[155] Over the ages, the same riddles appear time and again in different cultures, in different guises. It is even said that the ancient Greek poet Homer died of vexation because he could not solve one![156]

We are hard-wired to solve things. But we cannot solve a mystery. Mysteries are concealed, secret, hidden. There is immense power in concealment: that is why a mystery is endlessly fascinating. It is full of infinite possibility. Think of the mysteries of life, love, death, faith and hope. We give these things infinite meanings – personal, deep, relevant meanings. It is as if we want, or even need, mysteries in our lives. The more I contemplated sanctuary, the more I came to see it as a mystery.

Journal, April 2011, Kopua

I am not absent from myself yet, only from the world. I am a lost belonging, an idea that escaped from a small dark room, a loom, a womb, some place where things began according to a pattern. I am unravelling. I have to exhale before anything can happen. Allow myself to be empty, before I can be inspired.

We only see the wind in what it does.

The word mystery comes from Greek *mysterion* meaning initiation, which comes from *myein*, to close the eyes. A mystic is someone who closes his or her eyes to see. The allurement of mystery leads to insight. We wonder about and wander around a mystery until we are full of wonderment. Sister Jeremy Hall gives the best definition of mystery I know:

> … the inexhaustibly intelligible, the endlessly alluring, the depth of reality that invites us to enter again and again, to penetrate deeper and deeper, and that rewards us, not with a terminal or even a provisional 'solution', but with nourishment for our minds, our hearts, our spirits. God is mystery; the human person is mystery; love, whether

marital or parental, the love of friendship, or divine love is mystery; beauty is mystery; we ourselves are mystery to ourselves.[157]

One way to illuminate the depth of a mystery is by identifying some of the paradoxes concealed inside a mystery. Paradox masquerades, for a brief moment, as mystery. A paradox seems unsolvable and holds us, for an instant, in a tension of impossibility. When we 'get it' and see that it makes sense after all, we can have a rush of relief, even if the paradoxical idea remains uncomfortable. A good paradox is like a jolt to the brain. It jerks the mind backwards and forwards between opposite polarities of thought, until we arrive at enlightenment. A mystery, however, captures us forever within a tension of infinite possibility, as if we are held in a magnetic field. That is why a mystery charges us with energy.

Paradoxes concealed in the mystery of sanctuary

Uncertainty stabilises

There are good reasons to feel insecure in this world: promises are broken, love fades, disaster strikes, things are lost and people disappear. In a news-stream of disaster and terror, the world seems more frightening by the day. The only stability is in the certainty of uncertainty.

Once I lived alone in a small cottage on the edge of a beach. I thought I would never leave it, yet I did. Eventually, as the sea eroded the land, I became afraid of living there, so it ceased to be a sanctuary. I feel safe where we live now, three roads back from the sea, but I continue to watch the strength of some incoming tides.

Resistance traps

Journal, August 2009

I walked further than usual today and was shocked to see the damage further up the beach from the recent storms and high tides. I was looking at the ways people try to hold back the sea. They try to shore up safety with stacks of enormous boulders, or with metal cages filled with tiny rocks, or fortifications made of telegraph posts, high wooden walls, sandbanks filled with flax, and piles of metal rubbish. I can see the 'end effect', where one house is more fortified than the next so the sea has cut even deeper into the land alongside the weaker one.

None of us can hold back the sea, real or metaphorical. Any physical sanctuary against danger is only as strong as its boundaries.

Further down the beach one or two properties

had much looser fortifications: rocks with gaps between them, poles with trees and branches stacked behind them. Here, the sea can wash in and wash out again. Its energy is somehow dispersed. I wonder if the people who own these houses have accepted the inevitability of the sea's greater power, and instead of trying to be like King Canute, have learned to live with it, for as long as the sea allows them to.

The more we resist, the more we are trapped. That's what I learned from the beach this morning.

Change maintains

Journal, August 2006

I walked into Paraparaumu yesterday, and saw a big new house on the section where Jacqui's cottage used to be. They've demolished it. It must be five years since she died.

As I crossed the road towards the house I felt a grip of pain in my chest. It was just a moment, like a bite, and it was fear. I suddenly felt so vulnerable to be still alive.

My old beach cottage isn't there any more. Nor are the streets of my childhood. Everywhere things are demolished as part of regeneration. If I were not constantly changing, I would be dead.

Detachment connects

The less selfconscious I am, the more conscious I am of others. The more I detach from fear, the less my fear controls me. The less 'I' there is, the more I connect with God.

Frail ships

We are frail ships
that sail uncharted waters,
head in the eye of a storm
as if we were blind.
We make up maps,
as we go, for others
to follow. Coast into
coldest nights alone.
It is not the full moon
we seek, nor the sun.
Only that point of light
which walks on water.[158]

Containment frees

Imagine painting a picture on an infinite canvas, or composing music with an infinite range of notes. Imagine writing a poem with an infinite vocabulary. Now imagine creating something within a defined space. Which is more freeing?

I have almost always written poetry as 'free verse', which has very few elements of form. A couple of years ago, I decided that for one year I would write only in Shakespearean sonnet form, which has a well-defined and contained structure. I wanted to find out if I would still write freely from my heart. Once I was able to use the sonnet form with ease, I was freer than ever to write authentic poems.

If I stop words

If I stop words dissolving into ink,
and think instead of rhythm, form and rhyme,
will I relinquish that spontaneous link
of heart to hand, which sometimes feels sublime?
I write to listen, not to make a speech.
I never know what thoughts will fill the space
or what horizons could my feelings reach.
Poetry is a gift. A kind of grace.
I fear that tampering with the way I write
will block my path towards the secret door
through which I sometimes glimpse an edge of light.
Will sonnets hold me tight as I explore?
The page goes quiet. I take my pen in hand.
We only hear the truth in shadowland.[159]

Safety endangers

I want to love but not be hurt. I want to be mature but not be old. I want to belong but not necessarily to conform. I want to be cared for but independent. I want people I love to be free but am afraid to lose them. Just look at the *wants* in that paragraph! I want. I want. I want. What I am *really* wanting is not to be scared, for everything to be safe. But it isn't. I even have to let go of wanting to be safe if I am to feel sacred rather than scared.

Emptiness fulfils

Journal, July 2011, Kopua

Sometimes you have to just let go of it all, of everything and your self, and spend a day in bed, dreaming in circles.

Dream in circles, swimmingly, turn into spirals, kaleidoscopes, within and without.

Let go.

Let go of the struggle and see ideas float away like red balloons.

Make space to feel and cry with relief. And again. Not yet enough. More than you think is possible. Then, rest.

You have to let go of your body, stop clenching

your fists and grinding your teeth.

Let go.

Let go of worries and feel them trickle away. Watch vapour rising from the top of your head.

Swim if you want – be dizzy, dozy, warm. Snuggle down and cover your face with a quilt. Forget stiff upper lips. Weep.

Let go.

Let go and exhale. Breathe yourself out, completely. You need to make room for new breath. The space inside needs airing.

Lie back and wait. Just be empty and soon you'll receive new life.

Pain heals

I have to be willing to stand on the threshold of pain. When I long for and dread the same thing, I know that I am on the brink of connection with my true self. Tears tear me open, my heart breaks and love rushes in.

Darkness enlightens

Sometimes, writing comes to me in the night. It wakes me to let me know it's there. It is almost like taking dictation. One morning, however, I woke to find the bedroom strewn with pages and had no recollection of writing them. The pages were full of large scrawls – mostly, it seemed, nonsense. I felt uneasy, even afraid of this writing.

The first eight pages were full of numbers. I showed them to Doug, hoping a mathematician might understand them, but he said they made no sense so I threw them away. I kept the other pages but pushed them away at the back of drawer. I didn't get them out again until yesterday. When I read them *now*, they seem to make sense – as if I wrote things that I knew before I knew that I knew them:

In this world, we can only simulate the truth, draw lines when lines were never known, less named. Make long division when time did not exist & so we're short on sense.

In this world we can only see the obvious, make indirect connections. But underneath: all things, always, forever & before 'ever', ever was.

We can sing like angels, synthesise the symphonies, in a space where notes were not defined, when sound did not exist or even need to.

A time where there was none, no second's beat, no normalcy or containment, only space. When stillness could move & delineation made no sense.

A time before words had come to clutter our minds. When only shapes were friends, only shapes & even then, no form. No oceans, waves or sun, no night or day.

Before. Not even that, because no fore no after. Left with Be. The essence. Essential self. A state of being.

Where silence had not yet met sound. Where solitude had not yet met person. Where stillness had not yet met life.

An existence without opposites. So there were no comparisons, no compromise, no adjustments, no need for balance because no one could fall.

Once, we knew. Return to the when-where we just knew. Cast off, get rid of definition. It is certain but has an end, is finite.

Be where there is no need for certainty. Where safety is uncertain. Infinity is uncertain but safe.

Be still and know.

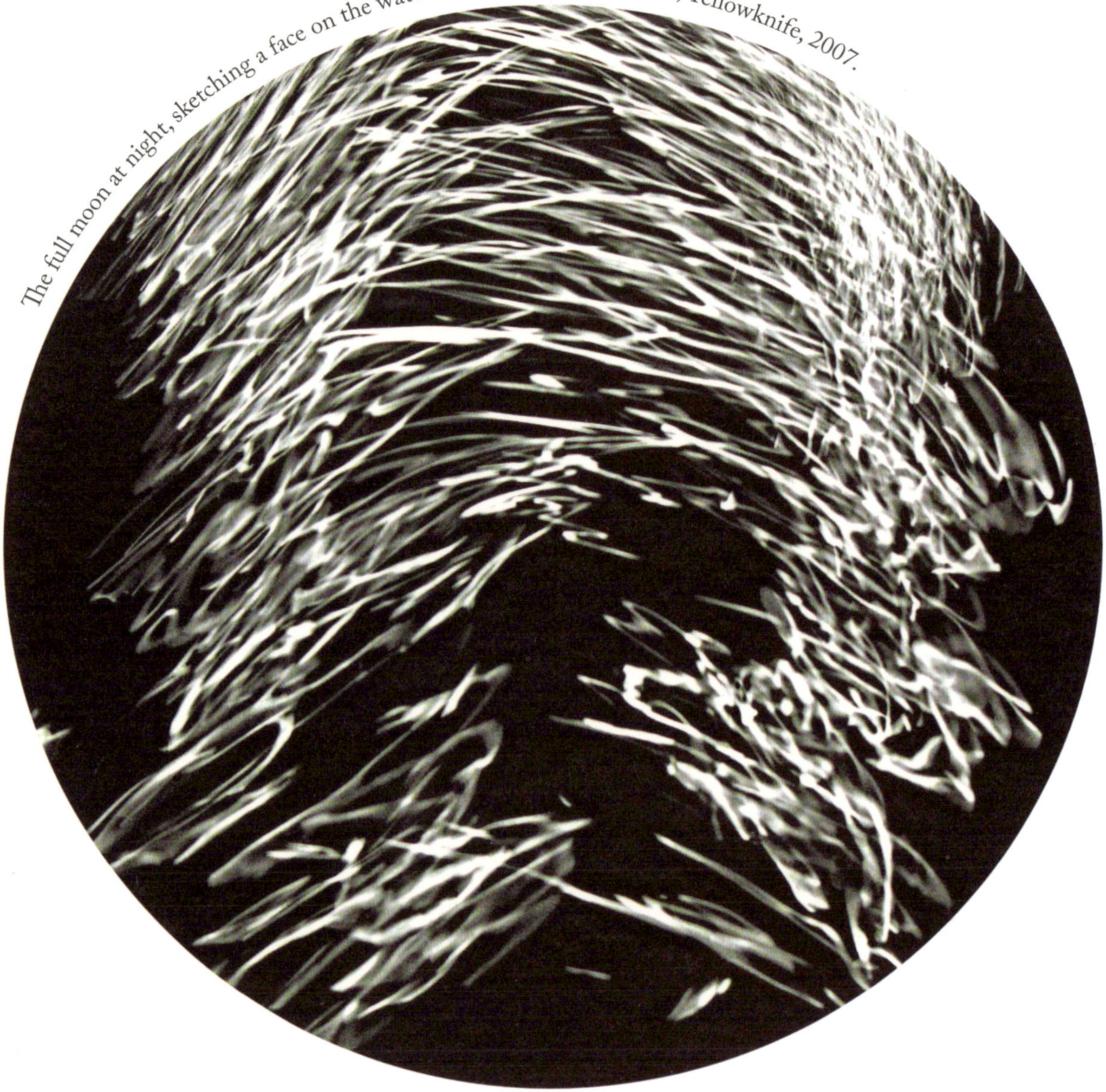

The full moon at night, sketching a face on the water of the Great Slave Lake, Yellowknife, 2007.

meaning

The least of things with a meaning is worth more in life than the greatest of things without it.

CARL JUNG[160]

I once had a colleague who said there was no meaning in her life, and she liked it that way. She didn't need it, hadn't looked for it, and it hadn't found her. She said things just happened and she lived her life in the present. I didn't understand. At the time I felt stupid, as if it were somehow smarter, more evolved, to live without meaning. All these years later I still don't understand. Perhaps she would say, 'What is there to understand? Life has no meaning.'

Meaning is as much about intuition as it is about logic. It is the point where heart and mind intersect. We feel so we sense. We think so we make sense. Meaning is the essence of sense. The word meaning comes from Old English *mænan*, meaning to think. Meaning is about making sense – thinking things through and sorting things out. I find meaning in my own life by thinking about the connections across time, seeing patterns and understanding significant themes. Significance comes through my senses, by feeling and discerning. Just as the stars point to the infinity of dark, so the physical signs of instinct – gooseflesh, shivers, catching of breath, sudden tears – point to something deeper within ourselves. They are reminders of the universe within and beyond us.

What matters is not the meaning of life in general, but the specific meaning I find in my own life at any moment – its personal significance. Without meaning, how could my life have purpose? Without purpose, who am I, where am I, and why am I here? The idea of my life without meaning leaves me breathless. Meaning inspires me.

Just as paradox can illuminate mystery, so metaphor, allegory, parable and story can amplify meaning. One of the greatest sources of inspiration in my study of Judaism has come from Chassidic tales. These were collected and shared with the wider world by Martin Buber.[161] These simple, illuminating stories about the early rabbis of the Chassidic Movement show how mystical ideas become love and joy in the everyday world.

We illuminate the meaning of our own lives by turning our experience into stories. This makes sense of our lives in a continuous way. It means we can see the future as part of our life. One of the finest examples of this is Viktor Frankl's book *Man's Search for Meaning* in which he described his experiences in Nazi concentration camps. He concluded that even suffering has meaning and that we have to say 'yes' to life.[162]

We are continually revising our personal narrative, adding new things and reinterpreting the past in light of the present or an imagined future. To illuminate the role of meaning in my own experience of sanctuary I have to return to my own story.

In the first section of this book I described how, in my early thirties, my life seemed to disintegrate. Almost 30 years later I felt a compulsion, which I could not ignore, to return to Yellowknife, Canada. This was the last place I had lived as a young woman with a future that seemed clear and safe. After that, it all fell apart and I never knew why. I didn't have insight. It was as if I had left something there and needed to go back for it. I couldn't say what it was or why I needed to return. All I knew was that I had to go back. So I flew to Canada and, with a friend, drove 3000 kilometres on the Mackenzie Highway from Edmonton to Yellowknife and back.

I still can't put into precise words why I needed to go back, but I know that revisiting was about understanding meaning in my own life and that it gave me an immense sense of peace. Although I did revisit places and people I had known, I didn't analyse past events. It was as if I went back to gather myself up – gather the parts that had somehow been left behind.

On the last night in Yellowknife, I walked alone beside the Great Slave Lake, watching the full moon sketch faces in the water. On the way back to the cabin I saw a wolf in the moonlight and we stared at each other, transfixed. Then, very slowly, it pivoted on its hind legs and disappeared.

Later that night my friend and I went beyond the boundaries of Yellowknife, hoping to see the Aurora Borealis for the last time. We were just about to give up when the Northern Lights illuminated the darkness in a sublime display.[163]

While in Yellowknife, I read Jed Rubenfeld's intriguing novel *The Interpretation of Murder*, which opens:

> The happy man does not look back. He doesn't look ahead. He lives in the present. But there's the rub. The present can never deliver one thing: meaning. The way of happiness and meaning are not the same. To find happiness, a man need only live in the moment; he need only live for the moment. But if he wants meaning – the meaning of his dreams, his secrets, his life – a man must reinhabit his past, however dark, and live for the future, however uncertain. Thus nature dangles happiness and meaning before us all, insisting only that we choose between them.[164]

I agree with Rubenfeld about meaning but not with his conclusion. Revisiting Yellowknife, I found intense happiness and profound meaning simultaneously. Day after day, there was joy in the present as I absorbed my past and realigned my future. I returned to New Zealand with a much deeper insight into who I am, where I am, and why I am here – with a much deeper understanding of the meaning of my own life. A few months after this trip, I began to write this book.

Journal, July 2011, Kopua

I wait for Vigils, with all the ones who have gone before, waiting. The space between dark and light is the mystery of creation. The moment I open the door and step into night I am in awe. I wax and wane in understanding, standing under the night sky, magnetised by the mystery of light-years. There is always a miracle in the dark: the intensity of constellations; the wind through trees; frost in moonlight. This is a place from which I can see both the rising and the setting of the sun and moon. Over the past 10 days there have been incredible torrents of rain. Again and again the sun has shone through clouds. It's like being in a rainbow, as Nesta would say.

I belong to the universe. I am the day and night, the sun and moon. The four winds blow through my heart and the oceans flow inside. I am growing in the earth. I am one of the flames in a fire. The word sanctuary is dissolving within me. It will soon be time to close this book, and let go.

miracle

The first time I saw the Northern Lights it was love at first sight. Yellowknife, 1974.

The first time an event occurs in nature it is called a miracle; later it comes to seem natural and is taken for granted. Let your worship and your service be your miracle each day. Only such worship, performed from the heart with the enthusiasm of fresh wonder, is acceptable.

THE BAAL SHEM TOV[165]

Inuit legends say that the Northern Lights are the souls of children who died at birth, or that they are torches shone by distant ancestors.[166] Some legends speak of spirits of the dead creating lights by playing ball in the sky. Dogrib (Tłįchǫ) people tell legends of the hero Ithenhiela, who climbed a giant tree up into the sky, and who, with his long fingers of light, is now beckoning the living to join him.[167] Cree say the spirits of departed friends are dancing in the clouds. An Algonquin myth says that when Nanahbozho, creator of the earth, had finished creation, he travelled to the north, where he remained. He built large fires, of which the Northern Lights are the reflections, to remind his people that he still thinks of them.[168] All these meanings converge on the miracle of spiritual life.

Scientists say that the Aurora Borealis is an interaction between solar winds and the magnetic fields surrounding the earth. I accept the scientific explanation yet still experience the Northern Lights as a miracle. They are not really incompatible at all – there is still no underlying explanation for the explanation. That night in Yellowknife something wordless happened. Now, I try to put words to it though none will do: my heart soared; I felt electrified; I knew that I was on the right path; I knew this was a significant moment in my life. A mystery given a personal meaning can become a miracle.

The word miracle comes from Latin *miraculum* meaning object of wonder. Usually a miracle is defined as something that breaks the laws of nature, and is thought to be supernatural in origin but there is a much broader definition of miracle as something that *occurs in nature* and fills us with wonder.

Like the Northern Lights, rainbows have been given many meanings. In the Bible, a rainbow signifies God's promise to Noah that he will never again destroy the world by a flood. In Greek and Roman myths, rainbows were pathways for the goddess Iris, as she carried messages down to earth from Zeus (Jupiter) and Hera (Juno). In Norse mythology, a rainbow is a bridge between Midgard, the human world, and Asgard, the home of the gods. North American Indian legends describe a rainbow as a pathway for the souls of the dead. Scientists explain rainbows in terms of well-known optical principles. Again, a scientific explanation does not unmake a miracle for me. I can even predict when a rainbow is likely to occur; yet every time it does I feel full of delight and wonder. It always triggers a sense of joy and hope.

'Mathematical mysteries', I am told, are not mysteries at all. They are just extraordinarily challenging puzzles that haven't been solved yet. Even when a mathematical mystery is solved, when the numerical patterns are understood and can be defined, the relationship between those patterns and nature may still remain a mystery. The mathematical laws of the Fibonacci sequence, for instance, are known but we still don't know *why* the pattern is observed so often in nature – petals, seed-heads, pine cones, shells and so on.

Just as paradoxes illuminate mystery, and stories amplify meaning, symbols point the way to miracles. Religious traditions are full of such symbols. Christian symbols include the crucifix, dove, fish and rose. Jewish symbols include the *mezuzah* (an encased scroll attached to the doorpost), *menorah* (candelabrum) and the *Magen David* (the Jewish 'star'). Muslim symbols include '*Allah*' written in script and the *hamsa*, a hand-shaped amulet with an eye in the centre of the palm (this is also a Jewish symbol). Hindus have the Om, which is made up of three Sanskrit letters that represent the Brahman, and the Swastika, which represents the infinite nature of the Brahman.

A circle as a symbol

When I am writing a book, quite early in the process I begin to imagine what it might look like. I have always seen this book as round, which unfortunately poses serious design problems! All the way through working on this book, I have been drawn to sketching circles to help me conceptualise ideas. I have played endlessly with patterns in circles. Doug even wrote a computer program to make it easier for me. My 'playing with circles' was much more than games. It was a form of contemplation.

A contemplation on circles

Womb, contained, closed, circular space, start of life. Whole, complete, encompassing. Circle of friends. Circle of life. No beginning and no end. Fullness and emptiness. Nothing and everything. The sun, the moon, stars, planets. Earth. Globe. The cycle of life. Someone's face, the shape of a head, eyes. Wedding ring. Ring – kingship. Celtic symbols. Mandala. Reading the Torah – the circling year. Cells. Seeds. Symbol of yin and yang. Zero. (Why was zero written as a circle rather than a dot?) Infinity. Unity. Sacred space. Female power. Circling, turning, wheel, spinning. Whirling dervish. Divinity. Mystery. Zodiac. The void, the essence of everything, enlightenment. To forgive completes a circle. I have come full circle.

A Love Story

Twenty years ago, at what I thought was the end of my marriage, I threw my wedding ring into the sea. I deeply regret that now but the course of love can be tempestuous. As I mentioned earlier, Doug and I did not divorce; we remained close friends and later resumed our marriage. However, my wedding ring was not replaced, which was a source of great sadness to me … until something miraculous happened.

Someone staying in our house while we were away thought he would do us a good turn by digging a small vegetable patch in the garden. Unaware that I was in the process of making a garden sanctuary, full of bluebells, he chose that particular place to put in a vegetable patch. Even though I knew it was meant as a kindness, I was terribly angry.

A few days later, still trying to deal with my anger, I was digging in the garden, turning soil, moving shrubs and spreading compost. As I was working around an old sweetheart rose, loosening its roots, I saw something metallic in the earth. At first I thought it was a bottle top, but when I picked it up and the soil fell from its centre, I realised it was a rose gold wedding ring. I put it on my finger and it fitted perfectly. I rushed inside the house to show Doug, who gave me a wry smile and said, 'Well, there you are. That *proves* we did the right thing!'

I have worn the ring as my own wedding ring ever since. There is an inscription inside it: 20th July 1925, H. Evans & L. Rallings. I have searched for a marriage record of these people – without any success. Sometimes I dream up stories of how the ring came to be in our garden, entangled in the roots of that sweetheart rose. It's a mystery. But, in my heart, I know the ring was meant for me, and that finding it was a miracle.

The red-billed gull is native to New Zealand. A flock flies over from Kapiti Island to Raumati Beach every day. In winter, I like going down to the sea to feed and photograph them. Raumati, 2003.

full circle

Full circle

> There is something you cannot find anywhere in the world … It is a great treasure, which may be called the fulfilment of existence. The place where this treasure can be found is the place on which one stands.
>
> MARTIN BUBER[169]

During the final year of writing this book, I kept trying to work out how experiences of sanctuary change me and my life. I began to make a long list of words about the gifts of sanctuary. It contained some of the most inspiring words in the English language. For example: freedom, discovery, authenticity, understanding, awareness, intuition, wonder, grace, inspiration, transcendence, transformation, creativity, compassion and hope …

I kept trying to connect these states of being into some pattern or logical progression. For instance, freedom leads to authenticity, which leads to understanding and awareness. That in turn leads to wonderment and creativity. And that leads to new life. But no amount of manipulating words brought a feeling of 'Yes! That's it!'

I stopped in my tracks. I had to accept that what I was doing was trying to force meaning rather than letting meaning emerge. I had resorted to old familiar techniques of logic and analysis whereas everything in my contemplation pointed to serendipity. I remembered how, in the beginning of the contemplation, I thought sanctuary was a shape-shifter. Sanctuary opens up endless possibilities of a better life.

My *anam cara* gave great attention to detail in her life. She did so many small things that mattered to other people. When she chose a gift, it was as if she became the person she was choosing it for; when she listened to people, she put herself aside to bring her full self to the listening. When I think of her, I am always brought home to this truth: it is the ordinary day that counts; the minutiae are life's core. Love is not in the great schemes and scenes of ethics and morality. It is this moment, this place, this person, this deed, this being. Life itself is the sanctuary. A life of love.

I am not *searching* for sanctuary any more. I know where it is. It is here, within me. I have it already. Although it is sometimes concealed from me, I am certain it exists, and that certainty is its greatest gift. It may be ephemeral, elusive, intangible and ineffable, but it is also permanent, identifiable, palpable and expressible.

Most of all, I want to reflect that sanctuary within my daily life. That means embodying sanctuary. Sanctuary is with the people I love, in the places I belong, in the wholeness of my mind, body and soul and in the seasons of my life. Sanctuary comes from 'the space within my heart'. Most of all, I want to mirror that sanctuary in my everyday life – in my thoughts, words and deeds. That means I want to be compassionate – show *chesed* (loving kindness) – to others. I do not want to do to others what I do not want done to me. So I need continually restore myself through the practice of solitude, simplicity, slowness, stillness and silence.

Once a week I stop for a whole day to value the sacredness of my life, and once a year or more I go on retreat for longer reflection on the sacredness of life. I read about other people's experience of life in books, listen to music, see art, do the things that inspire me and give me a sense of spiritual companionship. I have routines and rituals in my life that signify what matters.

What matters in daily life is to be compassionate to myself and to others. That means remembering that to be human is to be imperfect. As a monk once said to me, 'We stand up and fall down ... stand up and fall down ... stand up and fall down ... stand up and ...' There are times I will feel as I have lost a sense of sanctuary but it will return. When I am secure within, it is so much easier for me to be compassionate.

Journal, July 2011, Kopua

You are here. I am full of grace.

When you are without me, I am within You.

When I am without You, You are within me.

You are within me and without me. So I am never without You.

Rabbi Rami Shapiro, in his annotations of some Chassidic tales, illuminates this issue of apparent boundaries:

> 'Where am I?' This is the existential question Judaism places at the heart of human experience. Not 'Who am I?' but 'Where am I?' The difference between these two questions is critical. 'Who am I?' sets the self in isolation. To answer this question, you must turn inward. Turning inward, you separate yourself from the world around you. 'Where am I?' sets the self in relationship. To answer this question, you must turn both inward and outward; you must situate yourself in the world – both the world of self and the world of others. Indeed, to answer the question 'Where' you must drop the notion of inward and outward altogether and see reality as a seamless whole of doing, feeling, thinking and being.[170]

I have a vision of sanctuary as a circle, perfect and complete. Sometimes I still forget to protect my sanctuary – I make mistakes, have false starts, and fall down many times but I do enter sanctuary again. I also see that every time I experience sanctuary it makes me more likely to experience it again. So with each turn of life sanctuary deepens. It grows, like a spiral of ever-increasing circles.

In her autobiography, *The Spiral Staircase*, the religious thinker Karen Armstrong says, 'My life has kept changing, but at the same time I have constantly found myself revolving round and round the same themes, the same issues, and even repeating the same mistakes.'[171] This statement completely reflects my own experiences. And that is why there can be no conclusion to this book, only a point on a curved line.

Journal, October 2011, Kopua

I woke this morning thinking about gathering myself together. No Vigils this morning. The monks are having a 'day of recollection'. To re-collect, like re-member? To gather themselves together?

Maybe, after all, the meaning of sanctuary for me is that simple. I so much want to be gathered together in my life. To be integrated and whole, so I can gather with other people too.

Gathered together, together. Imagine that. That would be the ultimate sanctuary, wouldn't it? The universe, gathered together. Alone – all one?

It seems as if my inner sanctuary enhances my outer sanctuary – or perhaps the apparent boundary between within and without dissolves?

Maybe I do think too much. Perhaps all those people who've told me that were right. But it is my purpose to contemplate and write. I do my best to put it down on old bonded paper, with a watermark of tears, and imagine a monk stepping out of the eighth century to illuminate it for me. I see him standing there, by the gate, holding a lighted candle. I can hear the roar of the Atlantic around Iona in a storm.

Somewhere else, somewhere further off yet even closer, I hear the song of my soul. It is singing the Shema. What is it saying to me? What does it want me to know?

It is saying there is only love. No matter how distant, how damaged, how afraid. No matter in what guise it comes, there will always be love.

I am reaching an end to this book because it's all I am now. Am I living inside the book now or is it living in me? Is there a difference? Sanctuary is within and without. Like birth. Like love. Like life.

I have been in love with words. They curl around me like smoke on a distant day. I love them, so I cannot leave or say goodbye. But I cannot see when words are in my eyes.

When we love, we have to give away.

I am saying goodbye to something that has been a deep part of me for so long now, but in essence nothing is leaving. The words found me and will stay, because they have dissolved inside me now.

You are loved. You are safe. You are sacred.

All is silent.

בַּקֹּדֶשׁ חֲזִיתִךָ לִרְאוֹת עֻזְּךָ וּכְבוֹדֶךָ

So I gaze on you in the sanctuary
to see your strength and your glory.[172]

Winter willows in early morning light. Ranfurly, 2013.

appendix
glimpses of sanctuary

So many kind friends and acquaintances gave their time and energy to writing a few words about sanctuary when I asked them to think about what the word meant to them, or to describe a specific experience of sanctuary. Some of their words are included in earlier parts of this book, and in this treasury you can read more of their insights. Occasionally, I have divided up people's responses.

This appendix opens with a few definitions of sanctuary from those who shared their thoughts with me and then moves on to some glimpses of sanctuary.

Sanctuary is any place or situation where one can separate oneself from one's environment.

Within oneself: one can choose one's own time to be in sanctuary and to leave sanctuary. It is:

- A place (often but not necessarily a particular place) that can be visited, at one's own choosing.
- A place of security, safety and protection from the influence of others. A place where one can be silent.
- A place for quiet reflection about the things in one's life.
- A place to occupy oneself in personal matters without the restraint of time or the demands of ordinary concerns.
- A place to read or write without disturbance.
- A place of rest, of sleep and of relaxation.

With others: only you can choose to admit others to your sanctuary. One can choose to be alone, or to communicate with others in a like state of sanctuary. More than one might use the same place/time for sanctuary but to be left alone in sanctuary is to be respected by others.

DOUG HARVIE

I took the assumption that you were not referring to hiding in a church to avoid bandits … so perhaps it is the process of creating a mental vacuum, which then seeks to be filled with ideas, choices, solutions:

Sanctuary of MIND involves:

- Absence of outside influences, interruption from daily activities, stress.
- Distance but not necessarily separation from others.
- Openness – being courageous, challenging, flexible, creative, truthful.
- Thinking about deeper consequences, longer term, or maybe not thinking at all.
- Being self-focused, self-aware but not selfish. Heal yourself first. May be there for someone else's benefit.

- Sanctuary of PLACE involves:
- Quietness and peace but not always necessary – my music works fine. Running water is also useful.
- Being safe, secure, private, free to be whatever.
- Being comfortable – warm/cool (just right).
- Physically supportive.

- No distractions.
- Perhaps it can be an unusual place? Journey may be important for it to be a special place – to get distance, location (scene), atmosphere.

WARWICK HARVIE

For me sanctuary means many things. The sanctuaries throughout my life have been wide and varied. As a child, my home and family were my sanctuary. I was part of a large family (there were 12 children and I was the eldest girl). Everyone knew their place and being caught up in daily routine, life was simple, SAFE and uncomplicated.

It remained so for a long time – my mother and father being the main source of this place. Now they have passed away – all changes – but we, as a family, have maintained our bond even with the distances between us. My parents' legacy to us all is that we may not be demonstrative but we know our family love is strong.

My teenage sanctuary was babysitting. This was a great way to have peace and silence away from noisy family life and enjoy someone else's luxury – beautiful homes, their music, art – it offered a time to reflect and figure out what life was all about.

When I was a young mother, the radio offered sanctuary – Sharon Crosbie had such wonderful interviews. I was kept up to date on the 'adult world' while steeped in young children, housework. Sharon and her guests kept my sanity and, as an aside, I learnt a lot about books, politics and life in general, all from the inside of my home. Play Centre offered sanctuary too – that wonderful camaraderie of the people involved. We were all in it together, exposing our children to the world's offerings. There were all types of social interaction and learning through play – for both adult and child. They were the sunshine days. Wonderful memories.

Sports – running was my time out from the vagaries of life; it was my relaxing, reflecting time. The isolation of running alone early morning and late afternoons; fresh cool air; being part of the waking day or witnessing the setting sun: such freedom. Now I find sanctuary on the beach, walking alone on a long stretch of sand and listening to the sea, the simple ebb and flow; it's an opportunity to prepare for the day, to get rid of stale thinking and to bring back balance of being.

People – so many offer refuge. I am blessed that way: true friendship doesn't diminish with separation or time.

At times I struggle with where to from now, in this time of life when my children – adults now – are 'doing their thing'. I struggle with the letting go – the fact that the children are not my responsibility now; they need to find their way, discover their sanctuaries for themselves. I am blessed to have a dear friend, older than I am, with much wisdom who gently reminds me to live, laugh and enjoy life.

RITA KLAUS

Sanctuary for me, now that you invite me to reflect on it, has generally had two key ingredients: an absence and a presence.

First then, I find myself enjoying a sense of sanctuary when there is an absence of expectations and judgements. Too much of my life is spent playing to an audience, real or imagined. When I can get away from the gaze of others, and when I can put aside my own tyrannical expectations and judgements of myself, I experience the safety and freedom of sanctuary.

Presence, on the other hand, has to do with the 'sanct' part of the word, meaning sacred. There is something about coming to places that have a sense of the sacred, whether because they are beautiful, or wild, or because people have prayed in them for decades. I suppose for me the deepest, safest, most freeing sanctuary is in God's naming of me as his Beloved. That is the meaning of my name in Hebrew and that is where I find myself coming home, like the Prodigal in Rembrandt's painting. So places that connect me to this deepest place of homecoming are true sanctuary for me.

DAVID CRAWLEY

Sanctuary to me means a place of safety, refuge. It may be a place of quietness and spirituality, but not necessarily – as in the Kapiti Island bird sanctuary.

VIOLA PALMER

I think my experience of sanctuary, as I understand it, is best represented by my driving to a police station when a road rage guy was chasing me. I think its true sense involves an ultimate protecting power from a threat to one's person. I do not think a hiding place is sanctuary, as there is still no guarantee that I won't be discovered.

PHIL HAYWARD

I have been thinking about the meaning of sanctuary and have been astonished at its multitude of meanings. Like all abstract words it is very dependent on context. Without looking it up in the dictionary I decided its nearest synonym must be 'refuge', a place (or state of being) that provides escape from some other unwanted state of being. This may be temporary or permanent. It may be physical, in real time and real place, or it may be of the mind or spirit.

But essentially the word always seems to imply some sort of flight away from an existing situation that is threatening something of great value – life and limb, security/safety, peace and quiet, freedom (so many kinds of freedom!), privacy, understanding/acceptance, time to think; time and space to be creative, opportunity to be different. It may even be a place of escape from responsibilities, expectations and prescribed behaviours. So a local pub may provide sanctuary for a man who feels harried, demeaned or hopeless at home. But usually we think of such places of escape as quiet places: a study, library, the corner of a garden, bush or woodland. But it may equally be a place in which people can become so absorbed in an activity that all worries are blocked out: a bloke's shed, a music room, a movie theatre, a potter's shed, an art studio.

So what are we seeking sanctuary from/for? It may be a need to escape from thoughts, or a need to focus on thoughts uninterrupted.

Almost every attempt to be specific about what 'sanctuary' means leads to an equally valid but opposite concept. So, sanctuary may be:

- Temporary or permanent
- Purpose-built or improvised in response to need
- Accidental or reached only after much striving
- Familiar or unfamiliar
- Known to no one else or known to everyone
- A secret place or a public place
- A place to be alone or a place to be with others of like mind
- A place to be with God or a place to hide from God
- A place to think or a place to block out thoughts
- A place to find answers or a place to ask questions
- A place to find self or a place to lose self
- A place, a situation, an activity, a state of mind, free of day-to-day worries, irritations, distractions, fears.
- A place in which to be still or absorbed, totally comfortable.

JENNY SCOTT

It's something that you seek, or need to find if you are in trouble. The trouble itself could be a range of things – getting away from someone, something, a situation. By definition, therefore, it must be somewhere that is different from your normal surroundings. It could be a place – I guess I would think of a sanctuary as being somewhere safe and quiet. It could be a mental state … somewhere to let your mind go to relax – that special place with the waterfall and trees and sunshine.

RACHEL HARVIE

Sanctuary is a central experience. Sanctuary is a thing, a place, object, icon, book, music or silence that links you with a larger, greater world. This greater, larger world is full of meaning that enlarges and embraces your ordinary, limited life as a part of the whole. This world, or ambience, is *sanctus*, holy because it puts together all that is and can be: wholeness, holism where you may be and become fully yourself. This wholeness, holiness, is GOD as we say in traditional worship.

Holy, holy, holy Lord GOD Almighty, heaven and earth are full of your Glory. Sanctuary is most often identified with a special place or object (e.g. cross) especially a 'safe place' (cf. save, salvation) such as a church, nature reserve or your own 'inner room'. Sanctuary may also be anywhere at any time where you experience these new parameters: e.g. a moment of silence beside the sea. Sanctuary sometimes is described as a retreat – not as some place to 'hide away' but as a place to go forward into the larger, deepening experience of holiness/ wholeness that is sanctity.

JOHN MURRAY

I guess it means to me a physical place that offers shelter or protection from a storm. The storm can be a physical or an emotional storm in life: i.e. when one is going through a period of pain, one takes shelter or protection to alleviate the pain. I guess sanctuary is almost interchangeable with 'refuge' although for me refuge has a wider connotation than sanctuary; one could take sanctuary in a pub and refuge in a bottle. I guess the business of the physical place is important in sanctuary. Actually when I talk about life storms or emotional storms it perhaps seems more appropriate to take refuge in some other non-physical thing such as art. Sanctuary implies peace, rest and protection.

ERIC BIDDINGTON

I suppose that literally sanctuary means somewhere physical – the sanctuary of church (building) where safety is guaranteed. But in reality who can guarantee with certainty that a physical place of any description can really provide a safe haven? So, for me, sanctuary is a state of being where I am safe and free to be 'me' – warts and all!

Although sanctuary is a psychological place of 'safety and freedom', I do not mean I am looking for solace. I don't want or expect comfort, nor do I want to find an escape from harsh realities that come my way. As far as I am concerned suffering is part of the human condition. The safety and freedom that I want to find would enable me to meet such difficulties with emotional composure.

My experience of sanctuary has been neither permanent nor fully experienced. It has been approximate, relative or fleeting. But also it has been very meaningful. I have found sanctuary in: being alone, though at these times the safety is about being aware that I am part of a much bigger whole; in friends and family, when the relationship is one of mutual solidarity, 'unconditional' acceptance and common experience; and at times when I come to understand or see something with brilliant clarity which was hitherto seen only dimly.

Finally I think that a place of sanctuary is always one where I can feel a sense of love around and in and about me.

WENDY NORMAN

Belonging of place

The first image I get when I think of sanctuary is of inner peace. Tranquillity. A place to go where one can find this state. I think of the quadrangles of monasteries. I think of Chinese houses, where there are courtyards within courtyards; when you get to the inner sanctum it is the most serene place where even the screaming of the soldiers at the gate or the rowdy rebels (blame Pearl Buck and *The Good Earth* etc for the imagery) cannot reach you.

Sanctuary is a place where the outside world cannot touch you. No matter what is going on in there you are at peace with yourself; at one with your garden and therefore the environment, and I hope even connecting with your closest family even if it's not verbally. Sanctuary might also be something I would seek akin to political asylum. It is something I sometimes think I have been given by virtue of my family being accepted as immigrants here in an otherwise unaccepting world.

MYRA KERSNER

Quiet, solid monasteries in the mountains or other secluded places appeal, to me anyway, as a place of sanctuary, whether it is real or not. And that is so, despite my lack of any traditional religious belief.

I suppose a sanctuary is somewhere I could go to feel safe, secure, unthreatened, unchallenged, free from the day-to-day responsibilities of the world, and free too from having to justify myself. Sanctuary implies a degree of 'hiding' and I don't think that is a bad thing. I think we all need to hide from time to time, not only from threats and pressures in the physical world, but also from the threats and pressures we impose on ourselves. I suppose we hide from ourselves quite a bit.

For me a sanctuary doesn't have to be a substantial physical place. It may be a friend's house, a mother's home, or it may even be a vehicle. I know people who have taken to the road in house-buses, house-trucks and other vehicles – even just cars. Those mobile places of refuge are as much their sanctuaries as a friend's house may be to me.

In terms of physical places, a sanctuary can be whatever we want. I know a dell that my mother really liked – and I think some quiet time in such places give people some peace; some opportunity to recharge and perhaps to reflect.

When we were kids we used to have places such as 'forts' that were nothing more than a bit of a hole, a few 'ramparts' of dirt, and sometimes a form of camouflage. These were shared places and although there was a certain satisfaction in being in them, they weren't a sanctuary. But as a kid I had (as did many others, I am sure), places where I used to go alone, where I could feel secure. I don't just mean under a bed or something like that. I mean a different place where I could feel safe alone ... where I could relax. I remember I used to have a few places like this over the years. Usually they would involve being in the trees or bush and most often in quiet spots. Strangely, there was one spot I vividly remember where I felt very secure even though it was very exposed.

At the time we were living in what was then the Constable Street Fire Station in Wellington. I was about 10. Alongside the fire station is the town belt and it ends at a cliff overlooking the hill crest and curve in Constable Street. The cliff is quite steep, but it has smoothed-off pockets and 'steps' (at least for a 10-year-old) and if I sat on the side of the cliff I could watch the people and traffic go by without any danger of being interrupted. As I said, it was quite open, exposed to lots of eyes, but it was still a safe place for me, a private world. The fire station is now long gone but the cliff is still there. Whenever I drive by now I get a sense of warmth that comes from somewhere deeper than just a pleasant memory.

DAVID CURRY

I have been thinking about sanctuary and came up with three experiences, but one clear winner. The first two were:

1: Walking into my straw-bale home and sensing the love that went into its making.
2: Bed after not-too-exhausting exercise.

But the standout sanctuary for me was this:

3: The stillness of New Zealand bush with my eyes caressed by the curved green tones, my skin by coolness of the air and my spirit by the sense of being encompassed by the spiritual truth that 'in death there is life, in life death' – as the evidence shows all around me. For me this is a soul-lifting cathedral experience co-existing with such a sense of peace and contentment that I want to stop breathing and merge with the stillness.

SHIRLEY DUTHIE

There was a time when I was a teenager, around 15, when life was pretty tricky. My littlest brother had died, my stepfather left us in great financial strife, my mother was very ill, and we were suddenly living on the benefit. There were moments of tension for all of us, and plenty of weeping (between giddy dancing to 'Pass the Dutchie to the Left Hand Side'), but for me there was a place to escape to.

I had always had my horse, Pepper, and that was a great escape but very physical and requiring a lot of active concentration, so not really a sanctuary. Instead it was my time of discovering the earth, the grounding of soil on my hands and the absolute peace of weeding the vegetable garden, making compost, planting future edibles (life on the benefit was a little on the lean side, and I was a hungry teenager!). It was the place I ran to when I got so cross and frustrated that I couldn't argue any more.

I really took to the garden, found a place to let my thoughts slide around, mull things over. But the surprise was how my hands in the dirt passed the anger right out of me; it just uncoiled and wormed into the ground. Bliss.

I love it still. I have always had something growing: as often as possible it is food, because I know how good it is to eat what one has helped grow, but nowadays I get real pleasure from beautiful things: sweet-scented roses, tulips in spring, things that feel like luxury. In my garden I am at my most relaxed, content. My family know it. They are sending me out there all the time!

MIRANDA HARVIE

I had been nursing an abbot at the hospice where I worked. One day he patted the chair and said, 'Marie, sit down. Have you ever been to the monastery?' I said, 'No, but I'd like to go.' He said, 'Go, and you will never be the same again.'

Later, the first time I went, I visited his grave at the monastery. I was with a friend but asked the friend to go and give me some time alone there. I stood by the headstone and said, 'Well, Father Joe, here I am. Do what you want with me.' There used to be hedge there, and as I got to it, as I walked back, I stopped. This feeling came over me. It began at my feet and spread up my body and over my head. It was like being peeled – upwards. Suddenly I was freed of all burdens. I felt a tremendous freedom and light and all I wanted to do was dance. The monastery is my spiritual sanctuary.

MARIE PALMER

I go to the cathedral, for the cool, peace and quiet. I start to ease into another state, of openness to everything, and acceptance of what comes to me. My invisible muscles relax when I feel safe there. And it is bliss to feel safe, a kind of escape.

HELEN WATSON WHITE

For me, sanctuary is a womb-like place. I can find it by sitting quietly and visualising some special examples. It has been certain places on Mount Ruapehu, and an island with eighth-century Christian monastic ruins – an old church, graveyard and round tower – called Devenish Island, in Lough Erne near the town Enniskillen where I grew up in Western Ireland. There are other places of sanctuary I physically visit: such as the river Manawatu, specifically the bit that runs through the park, where there are mature trees and a remnant of bush. Kopua Monastery has become a place of sanctuary for me more recently. I discovered it about two years ago. I particularly like walking and sitting near the Stations of the Cross and looking towards the Ruahines. Sanctuary for me is a sacred space/place where I feel safe, loved, nurtured, accepted, and at peace with myself and in the presence of the Divine, which incorporates the male and female and creator.

JUNE LATHAM

There are a number of experiences from the old country and in other parts of Europe, especially in the Netherlands, because of a particular spiritual connection there, but the first thing that came to mind when I thought about sanctuary was Tawharanui beach north of Auckland. It has repeatedly provided me with a sense of the wonder of nature and the universe and a sense of peace and spiritual connectedness. Moving to a new country (in my fifties) hasn't been a bed of roses, so the sense of sanctuary to which I can return physically, and in my imagination, is consoling and restoring.

JUDI CLEMENTS

The meaning of sanctuary to me is solitude in a special place. My house and home provide a very special place for me, especially when I am the only occupant! One of the reasons for this is probably because I built the house 45 years ago and have great knowledge of the spirit of the house and gardens (that is, if houses and gardens have spirits). Tramping in the native bush is also a very peaceful and special time for me although I am rarely on my own. I think I am a solitary person who enjoys my own company, but I seek others happily and appreciate socialising. In conclusion, I am very happy when I can enjoy my sanctuary wherever, whenever!

MARIANNE JENNER

My personal sanctuary is my bedroom where I like to read and spend some ME time where I feel safe and private.

JENNY LIVINGSTON

I see sanctuary as a place, or state of mind where nothing can hurt or distress you. My home is the closest to it that I've got, but that's reasonably vulnerable – to natural disasters, drunk neighbours and so on. I am improving the odds by getting a small cartridge gas heater, light and stove! (Absolutely hate power cuts.) I guess it has to be a state of mind where you don't allow anything to ruffle your inner calm. Otherwise we're just butterflies at the mercy of any wind.

GLENDA FAWKES

Sanctuary: This word describes my home. I can go there at the end of the day, and rest and recover from whatever has gone on in my day. Thomas Hardy said: 'Every home is a monastery.

There, it is hoped, we can find solitude, community, beauty, nature, oratory and food. There, the spirit can be nourished and the body pleased with arts and pleasures.' What more can I say! This is my sanctuary.

PAT CUMMING

Some years ago while travelling to Greece, my husband and I took a cruise of the Greek Islands. Our last stop was Kusadasi, in Turkey. We were taken on a tour of an ancient city called Ephesus. There were a lot of excavations of old buildings and roads that showed how things would have appeared all that time ago. I had an amazing feeling of sanctuary there.

DENISE SAUSSEY

I think sanctuary can be in other people. My people found it with other people, living together and being safe together. There is also God coming down into that, sanctifying the people, the whānau. I think a lot of indigenous people have that experience, that understanding of sanctuary.

SARAH HANCY

My experience of sanctuary was in Italy with my father's family on a beautiful day in the most wonderful small village of Rubbio with lots of laughing and eating and of course drinking and feeling like I was in heaven.

TRISH FLYNN

Sanctuary means feeling happy and secure in my surroundings, and sharing this experience with people I love. An experience of sanctuary comes to mind from a holiday in Rarotonga five years ago. I was sitting on the beach having a glass of wine with my husband, mother, father, uncle and cousin, while my two little boys were building sandcastles. The setting was so beautiful with the waves gently lapping at our feet; we were lovely and warm, and we were the only ones on the beach. I felt very fortunate to be there, and being surrounded by such fun and laughter was wonderful. That was my sanctuary.

SIMONE GRIEG

Sanctuary means a place of safety, where you not only feel safe but you are also comfortable in yourself, where you are – in both place and head space – safe and free. I feel most safe at home where my family and I can be ourselves. There is no pressure to perform or be something else. We can just be happy in our own space knowing that we are free from the pressures of day-to-day life.

CRAIG FLEMING

Sanctuary is God, and being here in this community, but also when I get together with family and old friends.

BRIAN WALSH

My husband was in a hit-and-run accident, and after he came to from the coma he was totally disabled – mentally and physically. My sanctuary then was my faith and the support my family gave me. I was 26 and had a 10-month-old baby. My family put a safety-fence around me – like a sanctuary – and the security of knowing that I was well loved and that my parents would never let any harm come my way, made those feelings of hatred and anger disappear.

MARIE PALMER

Not something I have need of very often, but here are my thoughts:

When I separated from my first wife, in a state of general agitation and confusion, I found attending the weekly meetings of Nexus (a group for single, separated and widowed people) a very welcome oasis of calm. I reckon it took me most of three years to dismantle and completely rebuild my life, outlook, attitudes, values from the ground up.

Travelling a distance (plane, ferry, coach) is always a separate planet unconnected either to normal life or to destination. It's very valuable for taking that vital few steps back to look at life and where it is taking one.

Our 'other' life is spent in a campervan, wandering Europe in a gentle and exploratory way for six weeks at a time. It is immensely liberating, a simpler life free of home and family stresses – a sanctuary we almost prefer to 'normal' life; we return completely refreshed.

In terms of lifting the spirits (not a frequent need for me) heavy rock very loud does it very reliably every time (AC/DC, Metallica, Siouxsie and the Banshees, the Sex Pistols!).

I get something similar from the task of scanning old slides and films. I find it very uplifting to be engrossed in what were very happy times and some great photos.

Those of us with a parental home containing supportive, sensible, non-judgemental parents can find sanctuary there in times of stress or turmoil etc. I very greatly appreciated this at the time of my separation – and after. It was always a nice stress-free experience to slip back into the familiar home for a few days. This has been a model for what we now offer to our children, an offer which has been taken up on occasion.

CAMPBELL SAYERS

When I was young, I loved the hills, bush and open spaces that were available to me. I loved horses and was fortunate that living near a farm there was always a horse for me to ride. One in particular I now think was a sanctuary – a comfort – for me. She was a red bay mare and was my friend for a number of years. Often when childish concerns stressed me I shared them with her. I have a warm feeling now as I recall the times I have visited her in the paddock and stood with my arms around her neck, telling her of the hurt in my world, and she stood patiently listening and nuzzling me.

MARIE STOREY

Sometimes, though not as often as I should allow, I am transported to a self-induced sanctuary through the pleasure of living things. The loving, devoted eyes of my old dog, Charlie, used to absorb my worries and worldly cares. His absolute faith in me, his commitment, was a form of sanctuary. I knew I was always safe with him. Not that he could protect me from the world, but rather that he would be on my side, no matter what, and he gave his love and companionship without reserve. Sitting on the deck with an arm around Charlie and him leaning on me was one of the safest places in the world.

DAVID CURRY

What does sanctuary mean to me? Wow, that is one tough question to answer. I think I am yet to find it, but if I were to imagine what I think it would be like, maybe it would be a warm loving place, the sun would always be shining, I would be on a beach in a little shack and I would not be alone. I wish I could say I knew what sanctuary really was. I will be sure to let you know if I ever really find it. My son has lived with me now for the past six years and in a way he is my sanctuary – the thing that keeps me going and the true pleasure of my life.

JONATHAN RODGERS

A sanctuary for me is a situation that gives me a private retreat, where I am free from intrusion. It is also a state of mind, when I can enjoy the luxury of security – a true refuge from physical and emotional stress. I can achieve this situation emotionally when listening to certain pieces of music and I cite Sibelius's *Finlandia*. Poetry can also give me this private refuge or sanctuary. Saying aloud Louis MacNiece's 'Sunday Morning' does this for me.

BRIAN MEXTED

Books to me are a sanctuary. Not all books, but many. Those that can transport me to another world, make me feel that I am living another life, albeit just for a time, are just wonderful. Those that thrill with new knowledge or fill my mind with heart-pounding drama and adventure provide a 'transportation', and that itself is a sanctuary, at least for me.

The advantage of books (and films) is that they have the ability to quieten the other thoughts and stories that live in my head. The regrets, the hurts, the worries, the weariness, the self-recrimination; all of those things and more are put either on the back-burner or entirely out of mind while the story in the book or film allow a different focus and – if they are good enough – generate emotions and excitement.

DAVID CURRY

To me, personal sanctuary means a mental state in which I shut out, either intentionally or unintentionally, memories of unpleasant or unwanted thoughts or experiences. I usually enter such a state when I am in bed trying to go to sleep, and it usually has an associated fantasy.

When I was younger this fantasy often involved performing or conducting or composing some classical music in my head (usually at a level beyond that of which I was capable). At other times it involved some aspect of mathematics. Between 1977 and 1989 I might also have written computer programs in my head.

For some reason, which I cannot identify, this has seldom happened in the last 20 years or so of my life. My periods of sanctuary have been less frequent and usually involve 'the woman of my dreams', whoever she may be.

I guess one can say my periods of sanctuary involve having thoughts about my main interests to the exclusion of other thoughts. I do not recall ever having occasion to regard sanctuary as being a physical place although I realise that this could be a possibility for other people.

PAUL VINCENT

Writing itself can be a sort of sanctuary in that it helps to both express and contain some of our saddest feelings. When my first beautiful Burmese cat, Tortiegirl, had to be put down for fighting with Rose, I felt terrible guilt. Tortie couldn't have been re-homed as she was so very bonded to me and was terrified of other people, most unlike a Burmese. I wrote her obituary, which was published in the *Cat Fancy* magazine. She really was exceptional and I've never owned a cat like her before or since; it was like having a strange sort of miniature human in the house.

CAROL WORTHINGTON

Sometimes sanctuaries are places to recall – places of such peace that the memory itself brings calm. Such a sanctuary I found in the mountains with John, Anna and Ian. We had made the first ascent of Mount Bath and decided that the day to follow was to be a rest day. Our camp was under a large glacier rock that gave us shelter. It was a perfect day in that high alpine meadow. Anna and Ian went around the flank of Mount Bath while John and I walked down the high alpine valley. A small magenta hebe was in full bloom and with the celmisia and the large rocks it made a perfect alpine garden with no signs of other humans or even a chamois. The peace and beauty of the day filled me with awe – silently we walked.

I remember thinking, *absorb the perfection of the day*, recall this time if you need peace ever after, come back here in your mind until we live this time again. And so it *has* been, for in times of stress I have been able to return and recall the perfection in the peace of that day. So this experience, stored in memory, has been and continues to be my sanctuary, my haven.

DOROTHY PASCOE

I remembered an experience of sanctuary in my own life when I was visiting a playground I used during my younger childhood days, about 25 years ago, in Malaysia, my country. I remembered a time where I was able to release all energy, playfulness and creativeness naturally without elements of fear. We never heard of kidnap, molesting or bullying in those days.

WINNIE WONG

I have experienced sanctuary regularly in my life, as it often involves playing the violin (which I do for a living). I find it can bring about an inner harmony and sense of real satisfaction within my soul.

CHRISTIAN HALSTEAD

An experience of sanctuary for me was a couple of years ago when I was fortunate enough to do a cruise from Alaska to Vancouver. The ship we were on had music stations that had recliner chairs with footrests. I would frequently order a large latte from the coffee shop next to this area – sit back and listen to the music, sip my coffee, and watch the ocean roll by. I would flick through and choose different songs that interested me but on one occasion I listened to the song the person before me had listened to. The song was 'Time to Say Goodbye' sung by Andrea Bocelli and Sarah Brightman. The song is incredibly powerful and I would listen to it several times each time I came back to the music stations. Listening to that song gave me such an incredible feeling of peace and contentment. It is now one of my major favourite songs – I have downloaded it onto my iPod. Playing it gives me warm fuzzies and vivid memories of being on the cruise ship. I have told my family I want that song played at my funeral.

DAVID BRAZIER

In 1990 I was in the middle of a marriage break-up. I was living with my husband but had fallen in love with a colleague at the school where I was deputy head. We were having an affair but I was unsure what to do next. I wanted to be with Mike, but the enormity of leaving and hurting my husband, whom I was still very fond of, and giving up my home and a very comfortable lifestyle to step into a new relationship at the age of 40 was incredibly daunting.

For months, my mind seemed full of nothing but shall I, shan't I? Thoughts about my situation whirled round and round in my head; sometimes I was preparing to leave home, sometimes I was going to tell Mike it was all over. All this time I was doing the duties of a deputy head: talking to staff; sorting out students; organising this and that, and teaching. But this constant inner dialogue never stopped and I felt that I would never reach a solution and get back to normal.

One morning I felt particularly fraught, and I just needed to get away from everyone. The only place I could think of going where no one would find me was the medical room, which was a place where students could go if they felt unwell. It was very quiet in there, and on the wall was a poster that the school matron, a religious lady, had put up. It was a country scene, in the centre of which was one of those covered wooden bridges that are found in parts of rural America (like the bridge in *The Bridges of Madison County*). Underneath the picture were the words 'Give me that patience. Patience I need, Lord.'

I stood in the absolute silence and stared at the picture and the words for a long time – and it truly was a moment of absolute sanctuary when I was at peace, away from my thoughts, detached from my problems.

Of course, the experience didn't solve anything, but those moments gave me great comfort and somehow replenished me and I still remember that moment and how I felt, very clearly.

JANET SECKER

As my body is my temple, so it can be a sanctuary. For me sanctuary is peace and harmony, a place/state of 'being' or 'meditation'. Acceptance and trust are words that come to mind when I think of feeling/being in a sanctuary.

JILL STALLARD

Sanctuary is a place to retreat. A place I trust. A place to heal. A place where all my wounds, emotional and physical, can be opened and re-hurt then released or healed.

JILL DYETT

I have started road cycling in recent years. Quite often while out on the bike I can just let my mind wander – I think about all sorts of things and in a way this is a type of sanctuary for me.

DAVID BRAZIER

Sanctuary is a safe place either in nature or in my own home. At times it seems a place of sanctuary is around me, on the outside of me, surrounding me; at other times sanctuary is something that is very much connected to my inner being so it is an inner space. This means that a place of sanctuary could be wherever I choose to be.

To me it means time to myself, doing what I want, without feeling guilty about things not getting done or racing around after the kids. Taking time out of our busy lives. I love swimming. No one to talk to, no one to interrupt my thoughts, no one to put pressure on me. Only me and the water, which is very relaxing and weightless. Often I will swim and sing in my head and totally 'zone out' of everything around me.

JULIE AITKEN

For me, sanctuary is a physical place accompanied by a feeling. The feeling is a curious mix of peace, luxuriousness and reverence. God is present.

Expanding on that: sanctuary is a sacred place and a feeling of peace, safety, and tranquillity – harmony in body, mind and spirit. There is an absence of conflict and danger. It is a luxurious place and nature is always part of it. The Leith River and blossom, the hills and valleys at Paradise in Glenorchy, rocks and a cave at Pukerua Bay, macrocarpa trees forming a hideaway place on the Kapiti Coast. Love is strongly a part of sanctuary.

When I think of sanctuary there are common factors each time: my body and mind feel calm, I feel safe and contented. Deep love is always there; nature is always there. There is an absence of people. The only sounds are those of nature. My spirit is free, uncluttered and harmonious. The world feels beautiful. My life is fulfilled. Love is always there.

MARY GARD'NER

For me, sanctuary is the deep place where God is so close; that silence that touches my soul. Going to Kopua Monastery gives me the experience of sanctuary, so I take you into that experience. I enter the guesthouse and the peace and tranquillity encompass me and as I sit in my room the tears flow. I have come home.

I sit absorbing the silence, sitting at Jesus' feet trying to be Mary, from a Martha world. As I continue to sit, God brings words of songs to me: 'Come to the water', then 'Hold me close, let your arms surround me, draw me near, bring me to your side.' As the words continue I feel enclosed/enfolded in that love of God. This is followed by Jesus' words, 'You will never be thirsty again.' And we won't if we draw from the well of Jesus each day. The silence brings me peace, peace that flows through me and stays with me long after I have left Kopua. The peace that passes all understanding. The peace we can't explain, but know deep in our soul that it is there, and we are in sanctuary.

MAUREEN ELLIS

Sanctuary, to me, is spending time by myself talking to God. I have a time of sanctuary in the evenings reading my Bible and praying.

MARILYN THATCHER

For me, sanctuary is a place or state within, where my spirit thrives and it communes with the Divine. It is as simple as that. This sanctuary is available at all times to me.

ELLEN WOODS

An inner sanctuary: it dwells in the depth of my heart where I meet my Creator. I need silence through contemplation on God's love and through his Grace I can listen to Him. All that I do out of Love flows from this source (sanctuary) and is genuine, loving kindness and forgiving.

An outer sanctuary: my physical, sacred place that I use for personal prayer. It could be one that I set up in my bedroom, or the church, a walk in the park, on a beach. It is a quiet place where the environment is pleasant, peaceful and tranquil, suited and helpful to raising my heart, mind and soul and to praise God.

MARINA EDITH TU'INUKUAFE

Sitting outside the kitchen in the sun, my charge Natalie, whom I was babysitting, was asleep. This was a moment available for meditation – I forced myself into daily practice for a long time. It was a calm day and I tried to clear my mind. Then something really happened: suddenly a vision was before me.

It was unbelievably beautiful – very large – an angelic being of pure golden light – but there was an aura intermingled with blue. I had the impression that this was actually my own aura, which we were 'sharing', as it were, for the duration of the visit. The angel was very tall and I remember that the wings, unlike the angel wings in paintings, were of pure, insubstantial light. Nothing that I have ever seen in this incarnation has even remotely competed with the beauty of the effulgent being. The vision seemed to be before me for a long time. Then Natalie came from her bed, saying 'Grandmother,' and the angel no longer stood before me.

I wonder if Natalie's presence had anything to do with the angel's visitation? Maybe her presence, in all its purity, was the catalyst – the bringer of such a being so close to me? Who knows? Children are far more likely to be *au fait* with such beings than mature humans.

On the other hand – was it the guardian angel that I had so often asked to help me when in difficulties? Who knows? I can only say that the experience is one of the loveliest – *the* loveliest, really – that has ever been bestowed on me in this incarnation.

If only our eyes were open to 'the other side' more frequently!

BELINDA CRIGHTON

Sanctuary is the presence of indwelling God: motivated by love to return that which has been given. My Son, My Body, My Life, poured out for you all. With his holy body I find sanctuary. I return the love poured out in small humble blocks of time. Taking no book, or any distraction, I give my time and myself and I keep his body company in the prayer chapel. It is the least I can do.

TONY DAVIES

My appreciation of what I would call sanctuary (not a word that I use very often) is a place where one is free and able to BE. By this I mean a place where demands are set aside and the environment facilitates inner nurturing. It is not a matter of 'hiding away', of being in a vacuum. It is a place where the SOUL can be heard, fed, nurtured and given space to grow. I experience this sanctuary in several ways.

First, it is Kopua, where I leave aside my daily demands and give myself permission to BE, and 'go with the flow'. The quiet environment of countryside, bush, river and the people (generally) and the focus of God (Yahweh) are wonderful to behold. Without this focus, and my own spirit within, it would simply be 'running away'. I have been so blessed to be able to stay at Kopua.

On a shorter time scale my sanctuary is to stroll along a beach (open coast). I love the salt air, the motion of the waves and seeing others enjoying the environment. Often again I find a quiet prayer within in that place and hence sanctuary (however this is more in the nature of a respite).

At home, sanctuary is when I am of the right disposition and have the quietness to mentally leave aside pressing demands and meditate, pray, or reflect on scripture or some spiritual reading. Food again for the soul.

Sanctuary is not escapism, an example of which, for me, would be watching several TV programmes. Now and again it's fine, but for me it's 'nothing time'. I am very able to sit quietly and think, be aware, enjoy, without feeling I have to be physically doing something or be bombarded.

BRYAN WILLIAMS

The pure heart is God's sanctuary on earth. To our family, sanctuary means that nothing on earth can create a pure and clean heart suitable to be called the sanctuary or temple of God without the help and fulfilment of the Holy Spirit (Galatians 5: 22–23). It's hard to meet God's standard, but pray for forgiveness and seek spiritual empowerment to embrace your heart. Learn and live to pray all the time or at a set time. Learn to live to focus on him. Ask for his directive – remember to be with God. You are not on your own in this. His directive has to happen. In this way you will stay firm in your belief that 'what comes, will come'.

JONE, VANINA AND BASULU SENICEVA

My definition and personal experience of sanctuary is 'a place where I feel safe: emotionally, spiritually safe'. There is no specific physical place where this safety can be found. Sanctuary is the quiet, steady knowing that God holds me in the palm of His hand. In that place all loving, all forgiveness, all fulfilment, and all safety are found. There is no other place where this can be found in my experience. God, in His mercy, provides us with sanctuary.

HELEN HALLGARTH

Sanctuary for me is a feeling that comes from within. It can occur at any time, in many different places and with different people. However, it is generally a feeling I experience at home alone in peace and quiet. Being home alone is a rare occurrence, unfortunately. This inner feeling is of peace, love, safety, comfort, contentment and happiness. It can be in giving or receiving something dear to oneself.

My sanctuary is most often found while sitting in our spa, on our deck, at the end of a day. I also can experience this inner feeling while at a beautiful place created by God, such as the beach, a hill top, a field, a lake side, or spending time in God's house, a church. These are very spiritual places for me because I can feel his presence. Sanctuary is not necessarily a safe external place for me; it is an inner place, a feeling from within, a place where I can feel restful and at peace from deep within. This is when I feel connected and closest to my Creator.

One of my experiences of sanctuary was while I was grieving terribly for some contact from my mum shortly after she died. I was sitting one evening in our spa desperately wanting to know whether my mum could hear me or not. I prayed, 'Mum, if you can hear me please send me a sign.' Immediately a shooting star went by. This was the sign, I believe, from God or Mum. Now I sit out at night and talk away to Mum knowing she can hear me and whenever I see a shooting star I say, 'There goes Mum again.' This is sanctuary to me, the feeling of peace, love and comfort.

TRISH HOWARD

Sanctuary, to me, is when I go outside at night especially when it is a really clear sky and I just look at the constellations. I just let my mind clear from all the stresses of the day and I can spend 10 to 15 minutes out on the deck, then I go off to bed. My garage is another place when I'm looking for time out. I potter around doing odd little jobs, enjoying the time that I'm on my own, where I do what I want to do, when I want to do it, without having to be on a time limit set by someone else.

IAN WILLIAMS

I read Thich Nhat Hanh's *Miracle of Mindfulness* more than 30 years ago and tried to follow his recommendation to 'wash the dishes in order to wash the dishes': to give my full attention to what I was doing. I managed that occasionally, but found it difficult. My mind tends to plan what is next, or to go over something I could have done better.

I have found some situations in which I escape from this. Sometimes I can give my full attention to listening to another person; when I took a course on pottery at Pendle Hill I found that unless I gave my full attention to the clay on the wheel, I could not produce what I was aiming at, but when I did attend completely, the clay formed the bowl or the mug that I intended. Looking back I see a number of other activities that have helped me lose myself.

NEIL MOUNTIER

When I think of the word sanctuary I think of safety. So I suppose, to me, sanctuary is a place where I feel safe and at peace. Safe from what? Life's trials and tribulations: work, money, family, emotion. I can't think of a place that's sanctuary for me at the moment. But I had a dream once that sticks in my mind.

There was a man, who I didn't know, but he had such big presence. I couldn't see him clearly. I ran to him and he hugged me really tight. No words were spoken, but I remember I felt absolutely totally safe and at peace. Everything was okay and I woke feeling great!

It's quite interesting as maybe sanctuary isn't a physical place. Maybe it's something within ourselves that allows us to go anywhere, any time.

AILEEN DUNNETT

Sanctuary is achievable all the time – an inner peace despite possible hell all around. The choice that one has. Opportunities. Nevertheless, much of my life is subconscious. Anyway, sanctuary and non-sanctuary are complementary. Sanctuary is when you can't cope, standing aside, stepping back. Sanctuary is taking another route in the destiny of life.

SYD MOORE

Do you remember the Peter Sarstedt song that includes the words 'Where do you go to my lovely, when you're alone in your bed?' I have wondered about them over the years and come to the conclusion that they refer to our ability to transcend the present and to transport ourselves, through our minds, to other times and places. Sometimes this can be a time and place we don't want to be in, but other times it can be simply wonderful. To me, that is like having your own sanctuary, your own place of safety, in your head; even if it may be just wishful thinking.

DAVID CURRY

Sanctuary is connecting with mother. Sacred and joyful and beautiful. The peak of living, of being is any place you choose: alone or with people, on a hill, listening to music … it is sweetness, light, angels, being delivered out of the jaws, an epiphany, huge gratitude.

ANN NATION

Now, so much older, I have come to the conclusion that so often sanctuary is within myself. It is often not easy to reach because of all the anxieties and concerns that come into my life, sometimes unbidden, sometimes self-inflicted.

MARIE STOREY

Sanctuary is the place I can be within, without. It is a place of tranquillity of spirit, peace, safety, love, light, warmth. It is a place of being one with nature, close to God. It is the place where notions become ideas that have been quietly weighed. It is a place of reaffirmation.

FIONA REED

At its root, sanctuary is anything that allows me to feel real, or truly myself, or even just re-energised/recharged. That tends to mean being alone and with nothing calling for my attention or action. And being silent, too. However, there is an inbuilt frustration with that for me. While it is great to get time alone, without demands, it seems to imply that there's something wrong with the rest of my life, a fundamental dissatisfaction. I really long to be able to plug into this solitude and sense of being present all the time. I want to carry my sanctuary with me at all times, and if I can't actually stay attuned to that interiority all the time (which I can't) I at least try to switch to it when I become aware of it. That's what I focus on in my spiritual life. Basically that's what sanctuary means to me.

MIKE CLARK

My sanctuary takes many forms and changes from time to time depending on the reason for my need for a sanctuary. It is not necessarily a place and often it is a 'space' that I allow myself to have. I am not alone in my sanctuary, although at times I find solitude necessary. My sanctuary provides me with the time and the space to think through the issues I am struggling with or to celebrate something alone or with others. It can often be simply giving myself the time to enjoy an experience, reflect on an experience, or cope with pressures that are unbearable. My sanctuary can be a game of golf, sitting alone in a favourite place, or getting lost in a thought. At times it is a creative activity such as doing carpentry or planting.

RAJEN PRASAD

I would define 'sanctuary' as a place where one finds contentment and I can draw myself into that place inside my head quite readily without being in a specific place or shrouded in silence. For myself, I seldom seek either silence or a place of sanctuary. I think that might be the experience of having mothered a family of children who were literally space invaders. I mostly didn't object to that. In fact, I believe it created a state of sanctuary inside myself that I am able to retreat to.

Having found sanctuary in a place, or a state of mind, the next question is, what is one seeking in sanctuary? I said 'contentment' above, but actually it's more than that – contentment paves the way for a rich experience of joy of both soul and mind.

JULIA BUCK

My feeling of needing a sanctuary goes back a long way. In my parents' home there was quite a large cupboard and as a small child I used to get in this cupboard. It was my very own sanctum.

BRIAN MEXTED

I often say that my bedroom, snuggled into my soft cosy bed, is my sanctuary. It's the place I go to escape the rat-race world. The place no one is allowed to enter, unless invited! Failing that, there is always a bubble bath with the door locked. Sanctuary is the place I go to be still and be everything to myself and nothing to everyone else.

CAROLYN PERRY

For me a sanctuary is a holiday from sharing the often selfish reactions that I consider before I reach a position that accommodates others without ignoring my emotional and rational needs. It is a sanctuary because I do not have to reveal the often indefensibly selfish thought processes that I consider before working past them. (I hope!)

A sanctuary is silent, it is non-sharing, it is all accommodating; and, if it does its job, it is the home of 'research and analysis' that leads to compromise and progress, and, one hopes, happiness.

CHRIS LEE

I was in Canada, journeying through the national park region between Vancouver and Calgary. I stayed in several quiet lodges. It was early spring, before the tourist season started. Still very cold, still snowing at times – mainly at night – and I felt an energy in nature I had never experienced before. My trip was loosely organised so I could stay/move as I wished. I had no demands on me to do anything, or be anywhere to a timetable. For two weeks I was able to just be. The country was immense – as was the silence. It had an energy that enveloped and included me, resulting in a serenity of belonging I have never experienced before or since. All I wanted was to always remember what that felt like. I still do.

KATHY ANSIN

Sanctuary is a word that brings me peace: the memories of times spent alone in a silent, empty space, sitting in a pew praying, with the scent of wood polish and freshly baked bread and wine and grape juice, breathing in the palpable presence of those who have prayed in this space over the years. Sometimes sanctuary is a retreat; sometimes it is recharging for the work that lies ahead.

COLEEN KRISTULA

Sanctuary means love. I have found it in meditation, in quiet, peaceful moments with myself, and in shared silence in my relationships with others and nature. To me it's that inner sense of peace and love.

HELENA PALMER

Sanctuary is synonymous with peace and quiet, being safe from harm, knowing that I have in my small world those whom I love and respect and with whom I am on good terms. To cap it off, I would like to have something specific to look forward to – performing beautiful music, a special book awaiting me, a loving pet. To summarise: peace, safety, love and anticipation of joyful moments to come. Here's an experience of sanctuary: reading a wonderful book in bed with heavy rain falling on the roof and my beloved dog gently snoring in her bed in the hall.

JUDY MORLEY-HALL

Sanctuary always seems linked to a 'quiet, natural place, where one can be at peace from conflict, aggression and self-aggrandisement'. Other people could be there, but they would be committed to living in peace. It is also a place where there is time to reflect, to think, and to read and study. There would be music and simple, natural food … and a cat!

ALAN TRISTRAM

Sanctuary is a time of peace and being by myself. My sanctuary incorporates warmth, be it either a fire or the sun. Being outside among trees, sketching, with no other human noises!

ANDREA DENT

Sanctuary is a place or places to go and feel happy, safe, stress free. Maybe with good friends or even alone. Another one is travelling over a road on a dark, wet, windy night in my old house bus, its old diesel engine with its rhythmic beat and its headlights showing the way. It is very cosy and warm in the driver's seat and with my old cat asleep on the engine cover. The monastery is a place where I feel real sanctuary. It is a place of peace where I can forget stress and worry and be with God, and keep my life on the right road.

IAN McCLUNIE

For me there is also a form of sanctuary in deciding to live a simpler, quieter life – one without the constant competition, the rushing, the noise and the unsmiling strangers, and without the constant striving, intended or not, to obtain and use 'more'. So, my sanctuary is probably more within myself than it is a place. It is a peace and contentment that come with knowing that I don't really matter very much, and that what I do or don't do is not in any way critical to the greater workings of time and the world. My sanctuary is being loved and loving, and knowing the warmth and peace that come from that. Yes, I would like a place to go to sometimes, to hide away. But what I would find there would not be more than I have here, and now. I know I am lucky, for I am close to being truly content and at peace. And you can't ask for a better sanctuary than that.

DAVID CURRY

As a relative state, I have not yet had any real, physical, emotional or spiritual need to seek sanctuary, except perhaps unremembered, as a child. Therefore I am, so far, fortunate indeed that I find sanctuary in simple things enjoyed, like love of my family, friendship, music or good taste.

MIKE HARVIE

Sanctuary means, to me, a place where I am at one with myself and the world. For me it does not have to be a certain place. I have many experiences of knowing the feeling of being at one with myself. Lying in the sand being warmed by the sun and the gentle sound of the sea. Lying on some rocks at Lake Taupo feeling the sun again and listening to the birds. Taking time out to spend time with God, meditating. Listening to that quiet inner voice. Being at peace. Also when I am in church and, in worship with others, I can be taken to that holy place and know that I have entered into a sanctuary.

DALE DAVEY

Sanctuary is a beautiful ideal, with its hint of holiness, but too often in my life it is an elusive reality. It signifies a safe place to escape to and hang out, free from constraints of time and the cares, pressures and threats of daily life in the world.

I recently stayed – all too briefly – with friends who had a chalet for guests. Warm, curtained in but with a view if I wanted it, and with almost every need anticipated, I could sleep and wake when I liked, work or relax, choose to be alone or to rejoin people. I need to get back there soon. On a daily basis, the closest I get to sanctuary is to climb into a warm bed at night … but that can be pretty nice too.

ROGER STEELE

Sanctuary is peace and tranquillity, a safe haven, surrounded by trees with the sound of running water and the birds happily going about their daily business. The cicadas singing their song, and me, sitting in a big old swing chair while the sun's rays slip through the leaves and dance on my face.

CAROLYN PERRY

Sanctuary means to me safety and stillness – peace, tranquillity and solace. I do remember times of tranquillity and stillness, but often only in retrospect, as I am very busy. So, even when pottering in my garden, I am 'plotting' and planning. So, a moment to smell the roses (or daphne at this time of year) is just that – a moment – and the scent is enjoyed at the time but remembered as a time of tranquillity when I look back and think 'Gosh, how lovely!'

ANNETTE MORGAN

A personal experience of sanctuary is in personal retreat in a quiet setting – no demands, myself to myself – sheltered but inwardly spacious and nourishing.

Sanctuary is – being alone; no demands; no responses needed; calm, clear, quiet, silent, still; being with myself; being open to what is in the context of God: the universe; this land; green leafiness; outside; feeling safe; at rest; at peace.

BARBARA MOUNTIER

I first think of bird sanctuaries where birds, protected by external forces, are safe and free from predators. Birds in abundance – flourishing, cocky, confident, naïve – unaware of the big bad world. Not quiet, busy with birdsong – but all pleasant and positive noises. Not intrusive. One can do one's own thing. Birds belong, unencumbered by worry or any other burden. While it has boundaries, the sanctuary provides a true sense of freedom. My sanctuary is similar to that.

It is a place or space I can find or go to that someone or some other force has created. It seems important that it is not my own endeavours that create my sanctuary.

Sanctuary is a place you reach to from a place of danger, for example crossing a treacherous slope on a ski field. You are scared and adrenalin is pumping, but you can't stop. Finally you reach a safe place from which you can return safely home, determined never to go to the bad slope again.

Sanctuaries are places where people are meant to be and feel like they belong and are safe. Home can be (should be) a sanctuary, but sometimes, when for example kids are too much, one needs to seek sanctuary elsewhere – a café for example. Sanctuary can be temporary – a shifting space. It is the space where I feel safe and belong – where I can breathe out and, ideally, shed all worry and breathe deeply.

I don't think it is a place you can or should live in all the time – then it might become a prison. It has to be a place with genuine freedom to arrive at and leave.

TESSA THOMPSON

Some flowers from our garden for you. Raumati, 2014.

acknowledgements

This book had a long gestation and took a long time to write. Along the way I have been helped by many people. Some I can mention for particular things they did to support me, but there are a lot of people whose names won't be here even though they are a part of the book in my memory and heart.

I thank many friends and acquaintances who answered my questions about their understanding of sanctuary. Their names appear alongside their responses throughout the book and I am indebted to them for their contributions.

Then I want to thank people who have helped me understand and follow my own spiritual life. I couldn't have sustained my focus on this book without a period of solitude and silence for total concentration and I found this at Southern Star Monastery where I have stayed so many times in the last 12 years. I am deeply grateful to Abbot Brian Keogh and all the monks there, but especially to Father Niko Versley for his love as guest-master and mentor, and to Brother Tony Brown for all his kindness and our helpful conversations. Companions of Southern Star Abbey help the monks look after the guests, and meeting them has invariably contributed to my appreciation of Christian values. My special thanks to Graham and Sheila Macbride-Stewart who took me under their wings.

Many people have also helped me in my search to understand more about Judaism. I especially want to thank Barry Lent who opened the door to the Rebbe's wisdom for me, and my dear friend Myra Kersner, whose mother, like mine, was living at the end of her life in Carmel Court, a Jewish Housing Association facility in Manchester. Myra and I met there as visiting daughters and a friendship grew. I would also like to thank the residents of Carmel Court for being so loving to me – whenever I visited Mum I acquired numerous Jewish mothers, all looking after the daughter from New Zealand!

I wish to pay tribute to Rabbi Simon Jacobson, whose teachings about Jewish life and thought mesmerised me with meaning. I also want to thank my patient, kind and clever Hebrew teacher Bodil Rosenbaum and my fellow class members for all the smiles and shared determination to learn. A special thank you to Elisheva Parker for all her friendship and extra help with Hebrew.

Making a book is a slow and difficult process which calls for perspiration as well as inspiration. After four years of contemplation, I finished the first draft in 2009. It then went through two or three years of revisions. I could not have managed to get through this stage without my friend David Guerin, who freely gave me his editorial skills and edited the book not once but twice, so that I could twice send a manuscript out to a panel of readers for critical feedback. David is one of life's great lovers of language and it was marvellous to have his help at that stage.

The people who agreed to look at and comment were heroes and heroines. It was a big ask. Some of course fell by the wayside, but I thank them for offering; others stayed with me and gave feedback which was at times extraordinarily thoughtful and detailed. It all helped me. In particular I want to thank Margaret Thompson, Tessa Thompson, Christine Lenk, Janet Secker, Damian Ruth, Beverly Cresswell, Julia Buck, Leslie Clague, Linden Lynn, Ann Nation, Judi Clements, Jerome Carson, Shirley Duthie, Glenn Roberts, Marg Schrader, Shirley Murray, Syd Moore, Nick Antony and Judy Morley-Hall.

These are the kinds of friends who make writers want to write. They encouraged me to keep going, as did other friends. Thank you to Velma McClellan, Jennifer Bradshaw and in particular Kim Saffron who helped me with later editing and proofing.

When I heard that Otago University Press wanted to publish *Sanctuary* I was delighted. Rachel Scott has encouraged and helped me all along. I could not be luckier than to have her as publisher. She is one of those people who seems able to juggle a thousand ideas in the air and not drop a single one. As a writer herself, Emma Neale, my editor, brought great understanding to the task in hand. Her intellect and sensitivity made it a privilege to work with her. Fiona Moffat, the book designer, also designed *A Gift of Stories*, so I was aware of her calibre. She is a brilliant designer who knows exactly how to bring words to life.

In acknowledgments it is common practice to leave the person who is closest to you until the end. Then you say something like 'without his help … without his understanding my states of daydreaming … without his intellect … without his patience …' There is no doubt at all that without my husband, Douglas Harvie, I would not have written this book.

I am without him now as he died in January 2014. My anchor and my lodestar, I thank you with all my heart for our life together.

Julie Leibrich

RAUMATI, SEPTEMBER 2014

Bookcases look happiest when they are not too tidy. Raumati, 2011.

notes and references

Endnotes

1 Tzvi Freeman, *Be Within, Stay Above: More meditations from the wisdom of the Rebbe: Condensation and words* (Vancouver, Canada; Berkeley, USA: Class One Press, 2000), 215. See also Tzvi Freeman, *Bringing Heaven Down to Earth: 365 meditations from the wisdom of the Rebbe: Compiled and interpreted* (Vancouver, Canada; Berkeley, USA: Class One Press, 1996).

2 Aubrey Menen, *The Space within the Heart* (London: Hamish Hamilton, 1970).

3 See *The Upanishads: Translations from the Sanskrit* with an introduction by Juan Mascaró (Harmondsworth: Penguin Books, 1978).

4 Julie Leibrich, *Straight to the Point: Angles on giving up crime* (Dunedin: Otago University Press, 1993).

5 Julie Leibrich, 'The role of shame in going straight: A study of former offenders', in Burt Galaway and Joe Hudson (eds), *Restorative Justice: Theory, practice and research* (New York: Criminal Justice Press, 2006).

6 Julie Leibrich, 'The doors of perception', College Academic Address, *Australian and New Zealand Journal of Psychiatry* 31, 1997, 36–45.

7 Julie Leibrich (ed.), *A Gift of Stories: Discovering how to deal with mental illness* (Dunedin: Otago University Press/Mental Health Commission, 1999, repr. 2004), 187.

8 See H. Lapsley, L. Nikora and R. Black, *Kia Mauri Tau!: Narratives of recovery from disabling mental health problems* (Wellington: Mental Health Commission, 2002); *Life is for Living: 25 New Zealanders living with disability tell their stories* (Wellington: Office of Disabilities, 2005); Laurie Davidson and Linden Lynn (eds), *Beyond the Storms: Reflections on personal recovery in Devon* (Devon: Devon Partnership NHS Trust, 2009); Hannah Cordle, Jane Fradgley et al. (eds), *Psychosis: Stories of recovery and hope* (London: Quay Books, London, 2011); Georgie Tutt, *Caught Between Sunshine and Shadow: Living with and managing bipolar affective disorder* (Georgie Tutt, 2010).

9 Margery Williams Bianco, *The Velveteen Rabbit* (1922) (New York: Marshall Cavendish Corp, 2011), 12.

10 Julie Leibrich, 'Making space: Spirituality and mental health', Mary Hemingway Rees Memorial Lecture, given at the World Assembly for Mental Health, July 2001. For a copy of the lecture with complete illustrations contact Julie Leibrich: seacoast@paradise.net.nz. See also (without all illustrations) Julie Leibrich, 'Making space: Spirituality and mental health', *Mental Health, Religion and Culture*, July 2002, 143–62.

11 Chief Rabbi Sir Jonathan Sacks, *Letters to the Next Generation: Reflections for Yom Kippur* (London: Office of the Chief Rabbi, 2009), 30.

12 Julie Leibrich, 'Making space: Spirituality and mental health', *Mental Health, Religion and Culture*, July 2002, 143–62.

13 The three articles were Henri Baruk and Barry Lent, 'Moral psychiatry: Justice in the modern world in Hebraic civilization and in psychiatric practice, part 1', *Mental Health, Religion and Culture*, November 1998, 153–64; Henri Baruk and Barry Lent, 'Moral psychiatry: Justice in the modern world in Hebraic civilization and in psychiatric practice, part 2', *Mental Health, Religion and Culture*, November 1999, 47–58; Henri Baruk and Barry Lent, 'Moral psychiatry: Justice in the modern world in Hebraic civilization and in psychiatric practice, part 3', *Mental Health, Religion and Culture*, November 1999, 135–44.

14 Simon Jacobson, *Toward a Meaningful Life: The wisdom of the Rebbe* (New York: William Morrow, 1995).

15 Julie Leibrich, 'Standing still: Spirituality and sense', National Conference on Spirituality and Mental Health, Melbourne, Australia, March 2004: www.peoplewho.org

16 G.K. Chesterton, Chapter 5 of *Orthodoxy*, first published 1908 and accessible via the Gutenberg Project: www.gutenberg.org

17 Herman Wouk, *This is My God: The Jewish way of life* (London: Souvenir Press, 1992), 66.

18 For some good photographs of these places see Mick Sharp, *The Way and the Light: An illustrated guide to the saints and holy places of Britain* (London: Aurum Press, 2000).

19 A hurricane-level storm struck the west coast of the Hebrides on 11 and 12 January 2005. Serious coastal damage and loss of life occurred.

20 Julie Leibrich, *Shadow Friend* (Raumati Beach: Rosetta Press, 2009).

21 Julie Leibrich, 'In the mathematician's house' and 'The quietness of love' are in *The Paper Road* (Wellington: Steele Roberts, 1998). 'The count of everything' is in *Shadow Friend* (Raumati Beach: Rosetta Press, 2009). 'Tapestries' and 'How rituals are made' are in *A Little Book of Sonnets* (Wellington: Steele Roberts, 2012).

22 John O'Donohue, *Anam Cara: Spiritual wisdom from the Celtic world* (London: Bantam Press, 1997), 41.

23 Ibid., 16.

24 John Keats, Letter from Hampstead Heath to George and Tom Keats, 22 Dec. 1817, *Selected Letters of John Keats: Based on the texts of Hyder Edward Rollins,* Grant F. Scott (ed.) (Cambridge MA: Harvard University Press, 2005), xxii.

25 For example I read Roger von Oech's *A Whack on the Side of the Head: How you can be more creative* (New York: Warner Books, 1983), and various books on mind-mapping.

26 Griff Rhys Jones (ed.), *The Nation's Favourite Poems* (London: BBC Worldwide Ltd, 1998).

27 Lawrence Kushner, *The River of Light: Spirituality, Judaism, consciousness* (Woodstock, Vermont: Jewish Lights Publishing, 1995), 27.

28 A.J.J. Ratcliff, *A History of Dreams* (1923), (London: Senate, 1996).

29 Sigmund Freud, *The Interpretation of Dreams: The Pelican Freud library volume 4* (London: Penguin Books, 1975).

30 There have long been debates about the distinction between myths, legends, fables and stories. A very good analysis can be found in John Fiske's *Myths and Myth Makers* (1873) (London: Senate, 1996).

31 Alexsandr Luria, *The Mind of a Mnemonist,* trans. Lynn Solotaroff (New York: Basic Books, 1968).

32 Ibid., 159.

33 Alexsandr Luria, *The Man with a Shattered World,* trans. Lynn Solotaroff (New York: Basic Books, 1972).

34 John O'Donohue, 'Towards a poetics of possibility', *An Easter People: Essays in honour of Sr Stanislaus Kennedy,* ed. John Scally (Dublin: Veritas, 2005).

35 W.B. Yeats, *The Celtic Twilight: Myth, fantasy and folklore* (1893) (Bridport, Dorset: Prism Press, 1999), 1.

36 Bertrand Russell, *The Autobiography of Bertrand Russell*, 2nd edn, with an introduction by Michael Foot (London: Routledge, 2000), 171.

37 Alan Bennett, *The History Boys* (London: Faber & Faber, 2006), 56.

38 Walter Greenwood, *Lancashire* (London: Robert Hale, 1951), 294.

39 Emily Dickinson, poem number 1212, *The Complete Poems*, Thomas H. Johnson (ed.) (London: Faber & Faber, 1975), 534.

40 Peter Mark Roget (1779–1869) created the *Thesaurus of English Words and Phrases*, first published in 1852. Ebenezer Cobham Brewer (1810–1897) compiled *Brewer's Dictionary of Phrase and Fable*, first published in 1870. James Augustus Henry Murray (1837–1915) was the primary editor of the *Oxford English Dictionary*, from 1879 to 1915. The first part was published in 1884. Eric Honeywood Partridge (1894–1979) compiled *Origins: A short etymological dictionary of modern English,* first published in 1958. Henry Watson Fowler (1858–1933) wrote *A Dictionary of Modern English Usage*, first published in 1926, and was co-editor with his brother Francis George Fowler of the *Concise Oxford Dictionary*, first published in 1911.

41 Raymond Queneau's *Cent mille milliards de poèmes* (1961) (Paris: Gallimard, 2001) as cited in Denis Guedj, *Numbers: The Universal Language*, trans. Lory Frankel (London: Thames & Hudson, 1998), 31.

42 Daniel Barenboim, *Everything is Connected: The power of music,* ed. Elena Cheah (London: Weidenfeld & Nicolson, 2008, 5.

43 Barry Mazur, *Imagining Numbers (particularly the square root of minus fifteen)* (London: Penguin, 2004), 37.

44 A course given by Cantor Robert Esformes, a teacher at the Eilat Chayyim Jewish Retreat Center in upstate New York, at Temple Sinai, Wellington, New Zealand, 27 March 2011.

45 Rebbe Schneur Zalman of Liadi (1745-1812) founded Chabad, a branch of Chassidic Judaism. He is also known as 'the Alter Rebbe'. See Samantha Barnett, *The Quill of the Soul: The power of music*: www.chabad.org

46 http://crownheights.info/chabad-news/14000/the-jewish-people-owe-the-rebbe-a-great-debt

47 This quotation came from Jill Purce's introduction to chanting in an earlier version of her website: www.jillpurce.com

48 Personal communication from David Howard. See, for an account of the underlying research, David M. Howard, Jenevora Williams and Christian T. Herbst, '"Ring" in the solo child singing voice'. Reprinted by permission of the lead author.

49 David A. Cooper, *Silence, Simplicity and Solitude: A complete guide to spiritual retreat* (Woodstock, Vermont: SkyLight Paths Publishing, 1999), 54. Permission granted by Jewish Lights Publishing: www.jewishlights.com

50 Bren Kolson, 'In the spirit of Dene Dance: Why we dance': www.native-dance.ca

51 Julie Leibrich, *Shadow Friend* (Raumati: Rosetta Press, 2009).

52 Sark, *Transformation Soup: Healing for the splendidly imperfect* (New York: Simon & Schuster, 2000).

53 John Donne, 'The Good-Morrow', *John Donne: A selection of his poetry*, ed. John Hayward (Harmondsworth: Penguin, 1960), 23.

54 David Ziedan, 'A Sufi reading of *The Song of Songs*': www.angelfire.com

55 Simon Jacobson writes in 'Teruma: The lonely God', a weekly op-ed at www.meaningfullife.com: 'In The Torah, in *Shemot* (Exodus), God commands the people of Israel, "Build Me a sanctuary, and I will dwell among you." Exodus 25:8. This has been widely interpreted to mean that we, ourselves, are a sanctuary for God. When read closely, "Build *Me* a sanctuary and I will *rest* among them", it is very

obvious that the Sanctuary is not just a place for us to meet G-d, but also a place for G-d to "rest" His presence.' In the New Testament, in Corinthians, Paul says, 'Do you not know that your body is a temple of the Holy Spirit, who is in you, whom you have received from God? You are not your own.' (1 Corinthians 6:19–20).

56 Yoel Hoffmann, *Japanese Death Poems: Written by Zen monks and haiku poets on the verge of death* (Vermont: Tuttle Publishing, an imprint of Periplus Editions (HK) Ltd, 1998).

57 Julie Leibrich, *A Little Book of Sonnets* (Wellington: Steele Roberts, 2012).

58 V.S. Ramachandran, *The Emerging Mind: The BBC Reith Lectures 2003* (London: Profile Books, 2003).

59 V.S. Ramachandran, *The Tell-Tale Brain: Unlocking the mystery of human nature* (London: William Heinemann, 2011). Reprinted by permission of the Random House Group.

60 Ibid., 288.

61 Ibid., 292.

62 Julie Leibrich, *A Starling in the Northern Sky*, Commonwealth Short Story Competition 2001, CD published by the Commonwealth Foundation, 2001.

63 Pat Cumming, 'It's playtime now', in Julie Leibrich (ed.) *A Gift of Stories: Discovering how to deal with mental illness* (Dunedin: Otago University Press/ Mental Health Commission, 1999, repr. 2004), 49–55.

64 Julie Leibrich, *A Little Book of Sonnets* (Wellington: Steele Roberts, 2012).

65 75 years x 365 days x 24 hours.

66 Cecil G. Helman, Cultural Aspects of Time and Ageing, EMBO Report, Vol. 6 (Supp. 1), July 2005. It can be read at www.ncbi.nlm.nih.gov/pmc/articles/PMC1369268

67 But even measurement by the moon is tricky. The solar year has 365 days and from this we take the seasons, whereas the lunar year has only 354 days. Most lunar calendars – for example the Chinese, Jewish and Hindu – deal with this difference by adding a month in the year to catch up every so often. The only true lunar calendar is the Islamic *Hijri* calendar, which is not linked to the seasons.

68 Jay Litvin, 'A different kind of darkness': www.chabad.org

69 Rainer Maria Rilke, *Selected Poems of Rainer Maria Rilke*, trans. Robert Bly (New York: Harper Perennial, 1981).

70 David Steindl-Rast and Sharon Lebell, *The Music of Silence*, with an introduction by Kathleen Norris (Berkeley, CA: Ulysses Press, 1998), 116.

71 Abraham Joshua Heschel, *The Sabbath* (1951) with an introduction by Susannah Heschel (New York: Farrar, Straus and Giroux, 2005), 8.

72 Shlomo Carlebach, from *The Soul of Shabbos* in his collected writings: www.simpletoremember.com

73 [Author unknown],'What is *Havdalah*?': www.chabad.org

74 *Tashlikh* means casting off and the ceremony is usually performed on the afternoon of *Rosh Hashanah*. The sins of the year gone by are symbolically 'cast off' into flowing water – a river or the sea – and a prayer is read – a section from *The Book of Micah* that alludes to the symbolic casting off of sins.

75 Ken McLeod, *Wake Up to Your Life: Discovering the Buddhist path of attention* (New York: Harper One, 2002) 422.

76 Charles Seife, *Zero: The biography of a dangerous idea* (London: Penguin Books, 2000), 19.

77 Johannes Eckhart von Hochheim (1260–1327). The quote is from Book i, Sermon 17 and was cited

in *The Problem of Pure Consciousness: Mysticism and philosophy* by Robert K.C. Forman (Oxford: Oxford University Press, 1990), 108.

78 Lawrence Kushner, *The River of Light: Spirituality, Judaism, consciousness* (Woodstock, Vermont: Jewish Lights, 1990), 114.

79 Aryeh Kaplan, *Meditation and Kabbalah* (Maryland: Rowland and Littlefield, 2005), 300.

80 See David A. Cooper, *God is a Verb: Kabbalah and the practice of mystical Judaism* (New York: Riverhead Books, 1997); Adolphe Franck, *The Kabbalah: The religious philosophy of the Hebrews* (1843) (repr.) (Secaucus, N.J.: Citadel Press, 1979); Gershom Scholem (ed.), *Zohar: The Book of Splendour: Basic readings from the Kabbalah* (New York: Shocken Books, 1976).

81 The quotation of Rabbi Isaac Luria and its source is cited in Ari Solish, 'Containing the Infinite': www.chabad.org

82 Julie Leibrich, *The Biggest Number in the Universe*, illustrated by Ross Kinnear, (Auckland: Scholastic, 2004).

83 Julie Leibrich, *Nesta and the Missing Zero*, illustrated by Ross Kinnear (Auckland: Scholastic, 2006).

84 Pearl Buck, *New York Post*, 26 April 1959.

85 Anne Morrow Lindbergh, *Gift from the Sea* (1955) (New York: Pantheon Books, 1991).

86 Paul Tillich, *The Eternal Now* (New York: Charles Scribner's Sons, 1963). This material was prepared for *Religion Online* by Ted and Winnie Brock: www.religion.org

87 Jonathan Levin, *Walden and Civil Disobedience: Thoreau* (New York: Barnes and Noble, 2003) 85.

88 Robert Louis Stevenson, 'Henry David Thoreau: His character and opinions – Part 1', *Cornhill Magazine*, June 1880.

89 William Penn, *Some Fruits of Solitude* with an introduction by Edmund Gosse, (London: Constable, 1926), xii.

90 John Donne, Mediation XVII, *Devotions Upon Emergent Occasions* (1624): www.online-literature.com

91 Paul Tillich, *The Eternal Now* (New York: Charles Scribner's Sons, 1963), 17.

92 May Sarton, *Journal of a Solitude* (Boston: G.K. Hall, 1979), 1.

93 Anthony Storr, *Solitude: A return to the self* (New York: Free Press, 1988).

94 Aubrey Menen, *The Space within the Heart* (London: Hamish Hamilton, 1970).

95 Esther de Waal, *A Seven Day Journey with Thomas* (Guilford, Surrey: Eagle, 1992). I went on to discover Merton's own writing, and particularly love *Thoughts in Solitude* (1958) (London: Burns and Oates, 1975); *No Man is an Island* (1955) (New York: Harcourt Brace Jovanovich, 1978). Also see Patrick Hart and Jonathan Montaldo (eds), *The Intimate Merton: His life from his journals* (San Francisco: Harper, 2002).

96 John D. Barbour, *The Value of Solitude: The ethics and spirituality of aloneness in autobiography* (Charlottesville: University of Virginia Press, 2004), 183.

97 Jeremy Hall, *Silence, Solitude, Simplicity: A hermit's love affair with a noisy, crowded and complicated world* (Collegeville, Minnesota: Liturgical Press, 2007), 86.

98 Christopher Jamison, *Finding Sanctuary: Monastic steps for everyday life,* (Collegeville, Minnesota: Liturgical Press, 2006), 86

99 As summarised in Surah 97 of *The Qur'an*, titled 'The Night of Power'. Note too this summary from contemporary religious scholar David A. Cooper: 'He experienced many visions, ecstasies, and trances,

as is common when one does intense practice in solitude.' *God is a Verb: Kabbalah and the practice of mystical Judaism*, by David A. Cooper (New York: Riverhead Books, 1997), 52.

100 *Pirkei Avot*, which is generally translated as *Ethics of the Fathers*, is a collection of maxims and teaching about ethical principles of Judaism. It is a section of the *Mishna*, a fundamental work of Jewish law, which was authored in the third century C.E.

101 David A. Cooper, *God is a Verb: Kabbalah and the practice of mystical Judaism* (New York: Riverhead Books, 1997) 64.

102 Ibid.

103 Jalāl Ad-Dīn Muhammad Rūmī, *Birdsong: Fifty-Three short poems*, trans. Coleman Barks (Athens GA: Maypop, 1993).

104 Franz Kafka, *Letters to Felice* (trans. James Stern and Elisabeth Duckworth), Erich Heller and Jurgen Born (eds), (New York: Schocken, 1974), 155–56.

105 Emily Dickinson, 'There is a solitude of space' (1695), *The Complete Poems*, ed. Thomas H. Johnson (London: Faber & Faber, 1975), 691.

106 Rainer Maria Rilke, *Letters to a Young Poet*, trans. M.D. Herter Norton (New York: Norton, 1993).

107 Richard Mahler, *Stillness: Daily gifts of solitude* (Boston: Red Wheel, 2003).

108 Jalāl Ad-Dīn Muhammad Rūmī, *The Essential Rumi,* trans. Coleman Barks (New York: Harper One, 2004).

109 Janet Frame, *The Pocket Mirror* (London: Vintage, 1992).

110 Mahatma Gandhi, *The Way to God: Selected writings from Mahatma Gandhi*, ed. M.S. Deshpande (Berkeley: North Atlantic Books, 2009) 55.

111 Sarah Maitland, *A Book of Silence* (London: Granta Books, 2008).

112 Ibid., 47–79.

113 In *The Advice of William Penn to his Children Relating to their Civil and Religious Conduct* (1699): www.onlinebooks.library.upenn.edu

114 John Kelly, *Personal Prayer* (Kopua, Hawke's Bay: Southern Star Abbey), 54, 74.

115 Thomas Merton, *Thoughts in Solitude* (1958) (London: Burns and Oates, 1975).

116 For instance: Graciela Flores, *Trying to Do Too Much: Why multitasking fails*, Stanford Report, Stanford University, 2009; Greg Miller, 'How our brains make memories', *Scientific American*, 18 October 2010; *Headlines: The Neurological Foundation of New Zealand Newsletter*, Summer 2011, 2–5.

117 Leo Babauta, 'Simple living simplified: 10 things you can do today to simplify your life': www.zenhabits.org

118 Richard Mahler, *Stillness: Daily gifts of solitude,* (Boston: Red Wheel, 2003), 80.

119 North Carolina Yearly Meeting (Conservative) Faith and Practice, 1983. In *Quaker Faith and Practice,* section 20.27. This is the core publication of Britain's Yearly Meeting of the Religious Society of Friends. *Quaker Faith and Practice: The book of Christian discipline of the yearly meeting of the Religious Society of Friends (Quakers) in Britain* was approved by the Yearly Meeting 1994. This text is drawn from the fourth edition, with revisions and corrections approved 1995–2008.

120 Esther de Waal, *Seeking God: The way of St Benedict* (Collegeville, Minnesota: Liturgical Press, 2001), 62.

121 [Author unknown], 'The Nullification of the Commandments: Based on a series of talks by the Rebbe, Tishrei 5752 (September–October, 1991)': www.chabad.org

122 This is a combination of various etymologies.

123 Julie Leibrich, 'A mild mannered man', *The Paper Road* (Wellington: Steele Roberts, 1998).

124 Joseph Bailey, *The Speed Trap: How to avoid the frenzy of the fast lane* (San Francisco: Harper Collins, 1999), xxi.
125 Carl Honoré, *In Praise of Slowness: How a worldwide movement is challenging the cult of speed* (New York: Harper One, 2004).
126 Nicholas Carr, *The Shallows: How the internet is changing the way we think, read and remember* (London: Atlantic Books, 2010), 5, 45–46.
127 Eric A. Havelock, *Preface to Plato* (Cambridge MA: Belknap Press of Harvard University Press, 1963).
128 Nicholas Carr, *The Shallows: How the internet is changing the way we think, read and remember* (London: Atlantic Books, 2010), 120.
129 Joseph Bailey, *The Speed Trap: How to avoid the frenzy of the fast lane* (San Francisco: Harper Collins, 1999).
130 John Miedema, *Slow Reading* (Duluth, MN: Litwin Books, 2009).
131 Thelma Hall, *Too Deep for Words: Rediscovering Lectio Divina* (New York/Mahwah: Paulist Press, 1988), 3.
132 Jeremy Hall, *Silence, Solitude, Simplicity: A hermit's love affair with a noisy, crowded, and complicated world* (Collegeville, Minnesota: Liturgical Press, 2007), 35.
133 Ibid., 35–41.
134 Lawrence Kushner, *Sefer Otiyot: The book of letters* (Woodstock, Vermont: Jewish Lights Publishing, 1990).
135 Sten Nadolyn, *The Discovery of Slowness*, (trans. Ralph Freedman) (Edinburgh: Canongate, 2004), 199.
136 Carl Honoré, *In Praise of Slowness: How a worldwide movement is challenging the cult of speed* (New York: Harper One, 2004).
137 Cliff Crego, 'The ways of light and snow': www.cs-music.com. The original poem is in Gerrit Achterberg, *Alle gedichte: Verzamelde dedichteen, Volumes 1–2*, P.G. de Bruijn, Edwin Lucas, Fabian R.W. Stolk (eds) (Amsterdam: Athenaeum-Polak & Van Gennep, 2005), 292.
138 Wislawa Szymborska, from *Monologue of a Dog*: *New poems translated from the Polish*, trans. Stanislaw Baranczak and Clare Cavanagh (Orlando: Harcourt, 2005). The original Polish poem is in Wislawa Szymborska, *Chwila* (Krakow: Wydawnictwo Znak, 2002).
139 Yehuda Amichai, *The Selected Poetry of Yehuda Amichai*, trans. Chana Bloch and Stephen Mitchell (Oakland: University of California Press; 1996). The original Hebrew poem is in Yehuda Amichai, *Sha'at Hesed (The Hour of Grace)*, (Tel Aviv: Schocken Books, 1982).
140 Rabindranath Tagore, *Gitanjali (Song Offerings): A collection of prose translations made by the author from the original Bengali*. First published with an introduction by W.B. Yeats, (London: Macmillan, 1913).
141 Brian Turner, 'Sliding By', *Elemental: Central Otago Poems* (Auckland: Godwit/Random House, 2012)
142 Franz Kafka: www.themodernword.com
143 William Penn, *Some Fruits of Solitude* (1693) with an introduction by Edmund Gosse (London: Constable, 1926).
144 Julie Leibrich, 'The healer within', in *Folding Back the Shadows: A perspective on women's mental health*, ed. by Sarah Romans (Dunedin: University of Otago Press, 1998).
145 John Kelly, *Personal Prayer* (Kopua, Hawke's Bay: Southern Star Abbey, 2009).
146 Rabbi Nachman, *Outpouring of the Soul*, trans. Aryeh Kaplan (Jerusalem: The Breslov Research Institute, 1980); Aryeh Kaplan, *Inner Space*

(Brooklyn, New York: Moznaim Publishing Company, 1990); Aryeh Kaplan, *Jewish Meditation* (New York: Shocken Books, 1985).

147 Les Lancaster, 'The essence of Jewish meditation': www.bbc.co.uk; See also Brian Lancaster, *The Elements of Judaism* (Shaftesbury, Dorset: Element Books, 1993).

148 W.F. Bolton, *An Old English Anthology* (London: Edward Arnold Publishers, 1965). *The Seafarer*, ed. by I. L. Gordon (London: Methuen's Old English Library, 1966). *Ancrene Wisse Parts 6 and 7*, ed. by Geoffrey Shepherd (London: Thomas Nelson and Sons, 1967). William Langland, *The Vision of William Concerning Piers the Plowman*, ed. by Walter W. Skeat (Oxford: Oxford University Press, 1964).

149 Kieran Kavanaugh, *John of the Cross: Doctor of light and love* (New York: The Crossroad Publishing Company 1999).

150 St Teresa of Avila, *El Castillo Interior Or Las Moradas* (*The Interior Castle or The Mansions*) (1921): www.sacred-texts.com. See also a book of daily readings: Teresa of Avila, *Let Nothing Disturb You* (Notre Dame, Indiana: Ave Maria Press, 2008).

151 Julian of Norwich, *Revelations of Divine Love*, trans. Clifton Wolters (London: Penguin Books, 1966). See also a book of daily readings: *Julian of Norwich Enfolded in Love* (London: Darton, Longman and Todd, 1980).

152 William Johnston (ed.), *The Cloud of Unknowing* (New York: Image Books Doubleday, 1996). For quite a different translation (by Clifton Wolters) see *The Cloud of Unknowing* (Harmondsworth, Middlesex: Penguin Books, 1967).

153 Dorothea Brande, *Becoming a Writer*, with a foreword by John Braine (London: Macmillan, 1983) 166.

154 Albert Einstein, 'Mein Weltbild' (The world as I see it), *Ideas and Opinions*, ed. by Carl Seelig (New York: Bonanzo Books, 1954), 8 –11.

155 Natalie Arnada, 'A brief history of puzzles and riddles': www.articledashboard.com

156 Paul F. Baum, trans., *Anglo-Saxon Riddles of The Exeter Book* (Durham, North Carolina: Duke University Press, 1963), ix. The riddle that was supposed to have claimed Homer was this: some boys had been fishing and he asked them what they had caught. They replied: 'What we caught we threw away; what we could not catch we kept.' (I refrain from giving the supposed answer.)

157 Jeremy Hall, *Silence, Solitude, Simplicity: A hermit's love affair with a noisy, crowded and complicated world* (Collegeville, Minnesota: Liturgical Press, 2007) 83–84.

158 Julie Leibrich, *Shadow Friend* (Raumati: Rosetta Press, 2009).

159 Julie Leibrich, *A Little Book of Sonnets* (Wellington: Steele Roberts, 2012).

160 Carl Jung, *Modern Man in Search of a Soul* (London: Routledge and Kegan Paul, 1976) 75.

161 Martin Buber, *Tales of the Hasidim*, with a foreword by Chaim Potok (New York: Schocken Books, 1991).

162 Viktor E. Frankl, *Man's Search for Meaning* (London: Hodder and Stoughton, 1964)

163 An account of this trip to Yellowknife is on the internet. Julie Leibrich, 'A Letter from Yellowknife': www.peace.ca

164 Jed Rubenfeld, *The Interpretation of Murder* (London: Picador, 2007) 5.

165 Chaim Stern (ed.), *Gates of Repentance: The New Union prayerbook for the days of awe* (New York: Central Conference of American Rabbis, 1978, rev. 1996), 4.

166 I was told many such stories when I lived in the north of Canada.

167 James Mackintosh Bell, 'The Fireside Stories of the Chippwyans', *Journal of American Folklore*, Volume 16, 1903. Also available at www.archive.org

168 Dorothy Jean Ray, 'Legends of the Northern Lights', *The Alaska Sportsman*, April 1958; reprinted in S.I. Akasofu, 'Aurora Borealis: The Amazing Northern Lights', *Alaska Geographic*, Vol. 6, No. 2, 1979 (available at www.indigenouspeople.net)

169 Martin Buber, *The Way of Man and Ten Rungs* (New York: Citadel, 2006, 34).

170 Rami Shapiro, *Hasidic Tales: Annotated and explained* (Woodstock, Vermont: Skylight Illuminations, 2004), 190. Permission granted by Jewish Lights Publishing: www.jewishlights.com

171 Karen Armstrong, *The Spiral Staircase: A memoir.* (London: Harper Perennial, 2005), 341.

172 For the Hebrew see *Tehillim* (Psalms) – Chapter 63, on www.chabad.org. This phrase, in English, is known as Psalm 63:2 and the translation here comes from *The Psalms Grail Translation from the Hebrew* (Chicago: GIA Publications, 2000).